KINGDOM OF THE DEEP

KINGDOM OF THE DEEP

Colin Willock

SURVIVAL

ANGLIA
Television Limited

Boxtree

The publishers and author would like to thank the following sources for use of photographs on the pages listed:

SURVIVAL ANGLIA: Jeff Foott title page, 24, 34, 83, 84, 85, 89, 91, 96, 97, 100, 101, 105, 137, 139, 149, 154, 155, 165, 166, 168, 169, 171, 172, 173, 174, 175, 176, 177, 179, 181, 184, 189; Al Giddings 27, 150, 157, 158; Rick Price 33, 88, 123, 153; Annie Price 37, 38, 39, 40, 41, 42, 43, 45, 46, 47, 49, 50, 51, 115, 116, 117, 118, 119, 120, 121, 122, 125, 126, 127, 128, 129, 134; Dieter and Mary Plage 53, 56, 58, 59, 60, 61, 62, 63, 64, 65, 68, 69, 72, 74, 77, 80, 81, 142; Goetz Dieter Plage 55, 57. Alan Root 67, 70, 71, 73, 79; Sylvia Harcourt 75, 76; Dr F. Koster 78; Joel Bennett 86, 87, 102, 103, 106, 107, 109, 110, 111, 112, 113, 185; Peter Hawkey 90, 93, 95; Jack Lentfer 104, 108; M. Pitts 151, 160, 163, 182; Jeff Simon 161, 162; Colin Willock 183.

ARDEA: Ron and Valerie Taylor 9, 14, 15, 18; Ron Taylor 12; Valerie Taylor 16, 19, 20; Liz and Tony Bomford 10; François Gohier 23, 25, 26, 31, 32, 35, 131, 135, 141; P. Morris 29, 144; Ake Lindau 133; J. P. Ferrero 99.

THE BRITISH MUSEUM (Natural History): 132.

THE PHOTOGRAPHERS' LIBRARY: chapter openers.

First published 1990 by Boxtree Limited

© Survival Anglia 1990
Text © Colin Willock 1990
Line drawings © Boxtree Limited 1990

Design by Groom & Pickerill
Typesetting by Cambrian Typesetters
Origination by Culver Graphics Litho Limited
Printed and bound in Italy through OFSA

for Boxtree Limited
36 Tavistock Street
London WC2E 7PB

British Library Cataloguing in Publication Data
Willock, Colin, *1919–*
Kingdom of the deep
1. Oceans. Animals. Ecology.
I. Title
591.52636

ISBN 1–85283–100–6

Contents

Introduction

In 1969, when the Apollo 11 American astronauts were approaching the moon, they looked back at earth in wonder. Astronaut Michael Collins said afterwards: 'I'll never forget how beautiful earth looks, floating silently and serenely like a blue and white marble against the pure black of space.' The astronauts' photographs of this sight have now become part of space history. These pictures have given rise to the phrase the 'blue planet'.

The reason so much of earth looks blue when viewed from space is that 71 per cent of its surface is covered by the oceans. Yet while there are 326 million cubic miles of water, only 3 per cent of it is fresh, and most of that is locked up in glaciers and ice at the poles.

That earth has any water at all is the result of a series of fortunate cosmic events. With the exception of Mars, which shows signs of possessing water vapour and possibly ice at its poles, earth is the only planet in the solar system to possess limitless water. Earth's size, and distance from the sun, means water is retained in each of its three states – ice, vapour and, vital to life, liquid.

It is surprising to learn that earth has practically all the water it is ever going to get. Some 'juvenile' water (thought to be very similar in composition to the original 'issue', produced when the earth first cooled some 200 million years ago), is still added by eruptions and fissures on the ocean floor, and by volcanoes. But apart from these quantities, the planet is limited to the water received at the outset. It is continuously being atmospherically recycled as rain, snow and cloud vapour. Four fifths of this recycled water comes from the oceans and eventually returns to them.

The story begins 4,500 million years ago when great pieces of space debris were hurtling together to form the nucleus of the planet. As each asteroid struck, the explosion released volatile chemicals, including the hydrogen and oxygen needed to form water. Yet since earth was not then of sufficient mass to retain a thick atmosphere, much of the water vapour leaked away into space.

Hundreds of millions of years later, when the earth had been bombarded by even greater quantities of space matter, the planet was large enough to retain its own atmosphere, but it was too hot for liquid to form. Water vapourised on contact and became cloud again. Many millions of years passed before the surface had cooled sufficiently for water to start collecting in craters, presumably containing lakes of a thick, nauseous, chemical 'soup'. For thousands of years it then rained and rained, the sun never piercing the dense cloud layers.

Geologists estimate that approximately 4,000 million years ago there was a final bombardment of giant meteorites, some of them comets which scientists describe as 'dirty snowballs'. Some were big enough to make craters 1,000 miles (1,609 km) wide. The supposition is that these craters filled with water to become the first oceans, very different in shape from those we know today. But they contained the same water that fills our present seas and rivers.

Only in the last 100 years have we begun to understand not only the topography and geology of 'the deep', but also the life that exists within it. In 1872, the British research vessel *Challenger* set out on a three and a half year circumnavigation of the globe. It had previously been thought that life could not exist at great depths. *Challenger* brought back evidence in its trawls that life not only existed there, but was abundant. There were even species of quite recent origin.

The *Challenger* tested the waters to a depth of 26,850 ft (8.2 km) in the western Pacific, the greatest depth then known. In 1960, nearly 100 years later, the bathyscaphe *Trieste* descended nearly 7 miles (11 km) into the ocean. Dr Jacques Piccard, one of its two-man crew, found a flatfish 1 ft (30.5 cm) long on the bottom.

We know for certain that terrestrial life and the atmosphere itself are inextricably linked with the seas. The waters absorb most of the sunlight that falls on earth, swallow most of the carbon dioxide we increasingly produce, and create most of the oxygen we breath and increasingly pollute.

And yet when people talk of ruining our environment, we think almost exclusively of the less than one third of the planet that is above sea level. The astronauts' photographs of the 'blue planet' have perhaps achieved more than any other single factor in showing us that oceans and land are *indivisible*. This book is about that often neglected two thirds, the kingdom of the deep, the subjects of that kingdom among whom, if we care for our future well-being on earth, we should count ourselves.

Four thousand million years ago, the earth received a final bombardment of giant meteorites, some large enough to make craters one thousand miles wide. This painting by Michael Copus suggests how those craters filled with water to become the first oceans, quite unlike the ones we know today.

Shark!

L ike the crocodile, the shark got it right first time, or nearly first time. It is probably a coincidence that both are aquatic predators. Initially, they were so well adapted to their roles that evolution has only had to modify rather than radically alter the basic design. In fact the crocodile has remained largely unchanged for 135 million years.

The first sharks were successfully hunting the fishes of the warm Devonian seas 350 million years ago. Although they had not then acquired the perfect aquadynamic shape of the modern shark, no one today would have any difficulty in recognising them – sleek, streamlined hunters, armed with multi-pointed teeth, and capable of out-swimming the fish on which they preyed. It is unlikely they could manoeuvre as easily as their modern counterparts, because their paired fins were not much more than stabilisers. Some of them grew to more than 6 ft (1.8 m) in length. We know this because their fossils have been excellently preserved in the silt laid down by those ancient seas, notably along the banks and in the bed of what is now Ohio's Rocky River.

By the time the dinosaurs dominated the earth, some 150 million years ago, sharks had become more like the fish we now know. They could articulate their fins, giving far greater agility. Some grew to 9 ft (2.7 m) in length. By the late Cretacious period, 100 million years ago, the two principal orders of modern sharks were established; the lamniforms, consisting mainly of the large, active hunters; and the squaliforms, the smaller bottom-feeders.

The shark family does not end there. Since the day of the dinosaurs, two main offshoots have developed, the skates and the

A 15 ft (4.5 m) tiger shark has been known to swallow two 4 ft (1.2 m) dolphins. On the left flank of this tiger is a remora, or sucker fish. These attach themselves to the sharks by a sucker disc and rid it of parasites.

Rays, including the huge manta ray, which can measure 16 ft across the 'wings' are distantly related to sharks. Terrifying as the manta looks, it is a harmless plankton-feeder.

rays. There are also some poor shark relations known as *Chimaeras*, or rat fish, comprising 30 or so species. Scientists believe they became an off-shoot of the main shark evolutionary trunk perhaps as much as 350 million years ago.

Despite the fact that there are some 300 species of sharks, only a very few will attack swimmers, let alone eat them. Those that are man-eaters are so efficient that they give all sharks, quite undeservedly, a very bad name. Their ferocity also obscures the fact that sharks are fascinating creatures in many other ways.

Sharks and their relatives are different from all other fishes in their basic construction. Herring, mackerel, sole and trout, for example, all have a backbone and a bony skeleton. Sharks, skates, rays and their lesser relatives, the *Chimaeras*, are built around cartilage instead of bone. Cartilage is a flexible, semi-transparent material formed from a complex protein. The shark group is therefore known as cartilaginous fishes (*Chondrichthyes*). All the bony fishes are called *Osteichthyes*. Sharks are often thought of as a primitive fish because cartilage preceeded bone in the evolutionary development. Since they also lack an operculum, or gill-cover, which is present in bony fishes, the label 'primitive' is probably justified.

Yet primitive or not, they are superbly adapted for their job, which, in most cases, is to prey on other fish.

Sharks differ from bony fishes in one other important respect. Bony fishes have a swim bladder which acts like the buoyancy tanks in a submarine, except that it is never filled with water. This elongated bladder, which is an extension of the digestive system, can be filled with air to adjust the fish's buoyancy. Since sharks lack this piece of equipment they have to keep swimming to avoid sinking. The only exceptions are a few species that can inflate their stomachs with air to adjust their trim. Sand sharks probably have this ability.

The bigger predatory sharks might be compared to a modern fighter aircraft, having a streamlined fuselage filled with target-finding instrumentation, a comparatively small wing area, and enormous motive power. Indeed the power which comes from the undulations of the body and tail almost seems to drive the fish forward on its large pectoral fins, which, if they do not exactly act as wings, certainly play the part of ailerons and to some extent the rudder.

The instrumentation is concerned mainly with three kinds of signals or stimuli. Sharks have very large eyes which are almost certainly more effective at a distance than at short range, an obvious advantage when first sighting a prey. However, eyesight plays a far less important part than the sense of smell and the ability to detect attractive vibrations, such as those made by a wounded or struggling fish. The sense of smell is incredibly acute. A shark has a nostril on each side of its snout, divided so that there

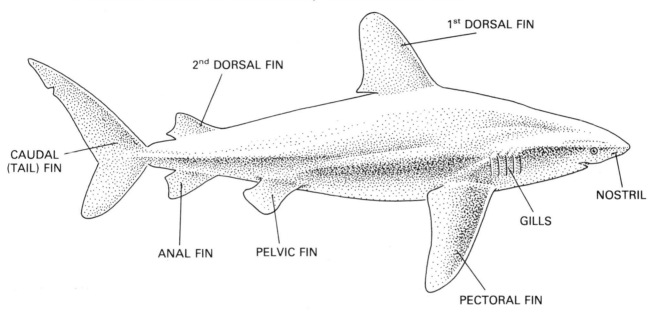

1st DORSAL FIN

2nd DORSAL FIN

CAUDAL (TAIL) FIN

NOSTRIL

GILLS

ANAL FIN   PELVIC FIN

PECTORAL FIN

is an inflow and outflow of water. The nostrils are connected to a sophisticated olfactory system that is capable of detecting the presence of blood in the water at 400 yds (366 m). No one knows exactly what a shark can hear, if anything. But then, like all fishes, their only need is to detect sound waves transmitted through water. Ears probably play a major part in maintaining balance.

The lateral line, the nerve endings down the centre of the flank, is common to all fishes and forms another important part of the shark's sonar system. In addition, sharks have pit organs distributed about their bodies. These are protected by scales that have a different appearance from the normal ones. No one is quite certain about the function of these organs, but they seem to be part of the sensory system, possibly giving added warning of prey or potential enemies. They may also act as a kind of radar indicating the presence of rocks, the nearness of the seabed, or even the action of

The shark's basic 'design' has not altered much in 350 million years. Sharks are superb hunting and eating machines. Unlike the bony fishes, they lack a swim-bladder with which to adjust buoyancy. If they do not want to sink, they have to keep swimming.

currents. Active hunting species have more pit organs than slothful, bottom-dwelling sharks. It has been suggested that the pits also enable sharks to taste. People attacked by sharks have sometimes reported that the predator first brushed against them, the pit organs possibly gauging their edibility.

In addition to this range of sensory equipment, sharks can detect electric fields. Prey fish sometimes generate weak DC currents. Experiments carried out with sharks temporarily deprived of the senses of smell and sight have shown that sharks can still locate a small flat fish buried in the sand, provided it is alive. Yet they were unable to find a dead fish in similar circumstances, presumably because it was not generating this current. It is thought that sharks can use such detecting skills to navigate by homing in on the earth's magnetic field.

The comparison between this ancient hunter–interceptor and the modern jet fighter is not wildly far-fetched. Like the fighter pilot, the shark is heavily aided by visual, sensory, auditory and electrical information. This enables it to navigate, avoid enemies and detect prey. Small wonder that we have come to fear this highly efficient predator.

Most of the bottom-living species are harmless to man. Some are extremely bizarre in appearance. One of the weirdest is the wobbegong or carpet shark. It resembles a roll of carpet, complete with tassels around the mouth. These algae-like growths make it look like seaweed when lying half buried on the bottom. However, divers would be well-advised to approach the sluggish bottom-dwellers with care. All sharks are immensely strong. One of the commonest, the nurse shark, has a particularly docile nature, although it looks like a small version of the traditional hunter-killer. It has only one snag – if it bites it hangs on literally until death. Even when dead, its jaws sometimes have to be forced apart.

This weird-looking creature is one of the carpet sharks. This species was named 'wobbegong' by the Australian aborigines. Like all carpet sharks, it is a bottom-feeder, living mainly off squids, molluscs, crustaceans and sea urchins. The tassel-like growths around its mouth help it to blend into the back-ground of the seabed on which it lies.

Fortunately, the nearest most people are ever likely to come to a shark is in the fish-and-chip shop. The dogfish, usually listed as rock salmon, is really a shark, albeit a small one. Other sharks come in far smaller sizes than the humble dogfish. *Squaliolus laticaudus* from the Philippines measures only 6 in (15.2 cm) in length when fully grown.

The diversity of sharks is not confined to their appearance. When reproducing they are extremely versatile. While most fishes broadcast the presence of their fertilised eggs far and wide, the majority being eaten by predators, in theory at least only one male and female need survive and breed to perpetuate the species. Since sharks are at the top of the food chain, they are far less numerous than their prey. They have therefore had to evolve a more protective and efficient method of reproduction.

Fertilisation occurs internally. Near the pelvic fins, male sharks have a pair of clasps. These are inserted into the female's cloaca, forming a channel for the sperm to reach her oviduct. Male sharks are usually smaller than their mates, which can be a lethal problem. Since courtship consists largely of seizing the female and giving her the equivalent of love bites a small weak male is quite likely to be savaged and perhaps killed by an unwilling female.

The females have three different methods of producing their young. Sharks can be viviparous (live-bearing), ovo-viviparous (the eggs hatch within the female's body), or egg-laying. Sometimes, a single species uses two different methods. For example, the female nurse shark can bear her young live or hatch them within her body, whichever seems best suited to local or prevailing conditions. Egg-laying species deposit their eggs in leathery cases, usually known as mermaid's purses, and leave them to hatch. The horn shark, which feeds on molluscs and sea urchins, lays its egg in a spiral case designed to wedge itself in rock crevices or lodge among weeds on the seabed.

The females of most species have nursery areas in which they produce their young, usually along the outer edge of the continental shelf in tropical waters where there is a plentiful supply of food. But there are exceptions. The tiger shark shows no preference for any particular breeding area, nor does it congregate socially by size or sex, as do many other shark species. There is an obvious reason why sharks of much the same size consort together, as with shoals of prey fish. Associate with larger brethren and you are liable to get eaten. This is particularly true where sharks are concerned.

The sharks that are most dangerous to bathers include the big ocean killers. They belong to the order *Lamniformes* though the lamniforms also include a number of small and harmless sharks, as well as the harmless but gigantic plankton-eaters. The dangerous ocean sharks in this order all have undershot jaws which do not look capable of making a big lethal bite. Nobody should be fooled by this appearance. They can all protrude their upper jaws below their snouts, a mechanism which pushes their horrific rows of upper and lower teeth into an ideal attacking position.

The great white shark (*Carcharodon carcharias*), villain of the book and movie *Jaws*, is rightly the most feared killer of all. Big specimens can reach 30 ft (9 m) in length and weigh up to 3 tonnes. To a mature great white, a man or a seal is just a casual snack. Unlike most killer sharks, they attack without any preliminaries. Their huge jaws, lined with rows of triangular teeth up to 3 in (7.6 cm) long, can easily bite a man in half, crush steel shark cages, and make large holes in, or even sink, small boats. Great whites

Sharks reproduce in three ways: they lay eggs (oviparous), hatch the young inside the female's body (ovoviviparous) or are live-bearing (viviparous). This white-tipped reef shark died giving birth but the baby held by the diver survived.

have even been caught with two adult sealions in their bellies, though they feed mainly on fish. They seem to have little preference beyond the fact that they like big mouthfuls. Great whites will chase fast-swimming mid-water species, but are equally ready to feed on sluggish bottom-dwellers including skates and rays. Little is known about this shark's breeding grounds and nursery areas. However, the species ranges as far north as the New England coast, northern California, and Canada, as well as Australia, South Africa, and even the Mediterranean.

The family to which the great white belongs also includes two other pelagic sharks with heavy dental armament, the mako and the porbeagle. Both are very large fish. The mako, the slenderer of the two, is quite capable of attacking and swallowing a 150 lb (68 kg) swordfish, complete with sword. The porbeagle is even bulkier. Both have to be rated as dangerous though they seldom are. They are also highly regarded as sport fish, particularly the mako since it can leap 15 ft (4.5 m) in the air after being hooked, a jump that demands an underwater build-up speed of around 25 mph. The maximum speed of a mako is about 10 mph faster.

This by no means exhausts the list of potential killers. Even very experienced divers confess to feeling a distinct chill when finding themselves alone in the ocean with a big hammerhead. Everything

A great white shark on the rampage is the most terrifying, and possibly the last, sight some divers will ever see. Unlike most other species, great whites give no warning of attack but simply come straight in and bite.

The Australian divers Ron and Val Taylor have probably spent more time than anyone else in the world photographing sharks and shark behaviour in the open sea. Here Val Taylor allows a white-tipped reef shark to bite her arm. Fortunately, she is protected by an experimental suit of chain mail. Nevertheless, the shark's jaws can exert a pressure of several thousand pounds per square inch.

about these sharks is normal, except the flattened and elongated head, with the eyes and nostrils set at the extreme ends of the 'hammer'. No one has satisfactorily explained the reason for the extraordinary shape of the head. Perhaps the visual siting of the eyes, and the organs of taste and smell, make it easier to judge distances when sighting prey. It has been suggested, too, that the broad, flat head act as a hydrofoil, giving greater manoeuvrability. A third possible explanation is that the electrical sensors in the head help the shark to pick up the bio-electricity sent out by stingrays, one of the hammerhead's favourite foods, as they lie buried in sand or silt on the bottom.

Some of the most conventionally shaped potential killers belong to the *Carcharhinidae*. These are the long, slim, fast aggressors that include the grey shark, the great blue, and the tiger shark. The tiger is definitely to be avoided and probably ranks second to the great white in terms of danger. Many of the maimings and killings blamed on the great white are almost certainly the work of a tiger. The largest specimen on record was just under 21 ft (6.4 m) in length and weighed 1,760 lb (798 kg).

Although it is said that more people die of bee stings each year than are attacked, let alone killed, by sharks, remember that more people are exposed to bees than will ever meet a shark. Annual figures for shark attacks are largely the result of guesswork, but the total for maimings or killings worldwide is probably around 500. A more realistic figure may be 1,000 because exact records are not kept. Clearly it is not the number, but the sheer, sudden, bloody terror of attack that gets most publicity.

Although there is not a 100 per cent method of remaining safe in the water, there are some techniques and rules which afford various degrees of protection to divers. Spear fishermen should get a struggling fish, and themselves, out of the water as soon as possible, as sharks home in very quickly on the vibrations sent out by a wounded fish. No one who is bleeding, and this includes menstruating women, should swim in shark infested waters. Sharks can detect even small amounts of blood from immense distances.

During the Second World War continuous attempts were made to find effective shark repellents, but without success. It has since been suggested to scuba divers that clapping the hands, releasing a stream of air bubbles or swimming towards an apparently curious shark may act as a deterrent. But none of these actions can be relied on to discourage a determined shark.

Chemical repellents that knock out other fish have been found to have no effect on sharks. Nor has the release of substances believed to be unpalatable to sharks, and mixed with purple dye, made much impression. Sharks have been seen swimming along the dye trail, possibly in the hope of finding something edible at the end of it. However, Australian bathing beaches are sometimes protected by shark-proof wire netting, which is probably one of the most effective measures.

For anyone unfortunate enough to be swimming for survival in the open shark-infested ocean, there can be few words of comfort. One horrific story from the Second World War should suffice.

In late July, 1945, the veteran American cruiser *Indianapolis* was intercepted and sunk 600 miles (965 km) south-west of Guam by a Japanese submarine. She rolled over and sank almost at once. Despite this, most of her 1,199 crew managed to abandon ship. Yet rescue boats did not arrive for four days. By that time there were only 316 survivors. Most of those who died had been killed by sharks who converged on the area in a feeding frenzy. Many of the bodies were horribly mutilated. Most of those wearing life jackets had had their legs bitten off while floating helplessly in the water.

Neverthless, people have survived the most terrible attacks, even by great whites. One famous case involved the Australian skin-diver Rodney Fox, who was competing in the South Australian State Spearfishing Championship off Adelaide, in August 1963. There was no warning. The great white shark bit him on the chest and back. He drove his fist into one of the shark's eyeballs; as he did so his right arm slipped into the shark's jaws. The shark came in again and dragged him down by his diving belt, which the shark's teeth fortunately severed. Released, he floated to the surface, horribly mutilated. When rescuers hauled him into a boat they saw that his rib cage, the upper part of his stomach, and lungs were exposed. One lung had been punctured, the flesh was stripped from his right arm, and some ribs had been crushed. Incredibly,

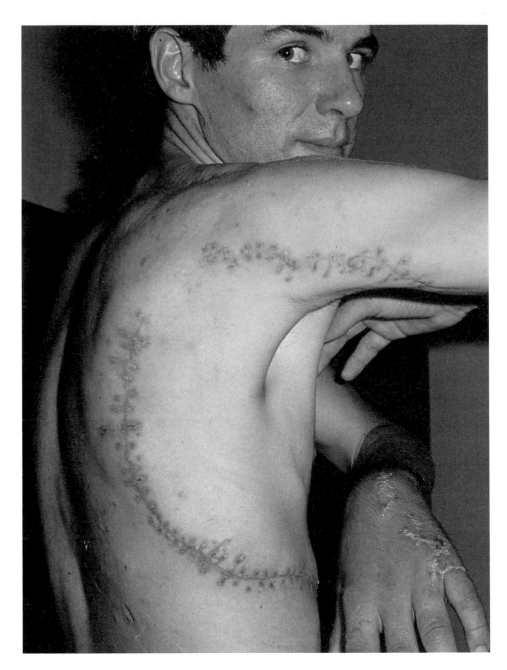

The great white shark that attacked Rodney Fox while he was competing in a spear-fishing championship off Adelaide in 1963 exposed his rib cage, stomach and lungs. Incredibly, Fox survived. Twenty seven years later he is one of the foremost campaigners for protection of the great white, maintaining that in some areas it is being wiped out by sport fishermen.

Fox survived, but it took 462 stitches to sew him together. He carried on diving after his recovery!

Two scientists, Don Nelson and Richard Johnson, have carried out successful research, mainly on white-tip and grey reef sharks, in the Pacific at Rangiroa Island. They have discovered that with certain species, notably the grey reef shark, clear warning of a possible attack is given by the shark's swimming posture or agonistic display. A grey reef, when ready to attack, starts swimming erratically with its back arched, snout raised, and pelvic fins depressed. This swimming posture results in a rolling motion through the water. Unfortunately by the time any swimmer has noticed these signals it is unlikely he or she will have the time or means to get out of the water. And if anyone needs further convincing that a shark attack is to be avoided at all costs, it should be added that bite-meter tests carried out on a big mako established that its jaws exerted a pressure of 8,000 lb per sq in (3,629 kg per 6.45 cm^2).

Another shark attack victim, Henri Bource, displays a great white shark mutilated by another of its kind while being played by a big game angler. Bource himself lost a leg to shark attack in Australian waters. Four years later, he was again attacked and the shark took his artificial limb.

Humpbacks – The Gentle Giants

In the beginning, life emerged from the sea to colonise the land. At some time, unimaginably long ago, the ancestors of four groups of mammals reversed the process. The four groups were: the sea otters; seals and walruses; sea cows, of which only two species, the manatee and the dugong still exist; and whales. Why these creatures returned to the sea is not entirely clear since they had been terrestrial for a very long time. The most likely explanation is that life on land was becoming too competitive. A return to the sea seemed the only answer. However, it was not a sudden return, any more than their initial adaptation to the demands of land life had been sudden.

The mammals had benefited from land life by acquiring sharper brains than fishes. But they also suffered from having evolved lungs for breathing, a distinct disadvantage when living in water.

When it came to the development of the brain there seems little doubt that the *Cetaceans* (the whales, dolphins and porpoises) came out top. The whales evolved through two main groups, known as the *Odontoceti*, or toothed whales, and the *Mysticeti*, the baleen or whalebone whales. The toothed wales include the dolphins – a term for a small whale – of which the *Orca* or killer whale is one; the bottle-nosed or beaked whales; the freshwater dolphins; the porpoises; the beluga, or white whale; the narwhal, which has a single jutting tooth several feet long, like a unicorn's horn; and the giant, the sperm whale. None of these has teeth of varied shape, unlike land mammals, for munching. Their teeth are sharp-pointed to grasp and hold slippery prey such as small fish and, in the sperm whale's case, giant squid.

The bottle-nose dolphin is the cetacean that appears to enjoy man's company more than any other. There are well-authenticated stories of dolphins haunting bays to play with divers and even helping swimmers in difficulty.

The baleen whales feed quite differently, cruising through the ocean with open mouths scooping up vast quantities of plankton, notably euphausids, shrimplike creatures collectively known as krill. To filter this food out of the intake of hundreds of gallons of water, the toothless whales are equipped with baleen or whalebone filters in their throats. The toothless whales include the largest animal on earth, in fact the largest known animal, and that includes the dinosaurs. A mature blue whale can weigh as much as 1,600 men, 150 cows, or 25 elephants! The other main representatives of this group are the right whales, grey whales, rorquals, and humpbacks. They are all remarkably interesting creatures although one of the smaller of the great whales, at around 45 tonnes, is probably the most interesting.

The humpback differs in appearance from all other whales by the great length of its flippers. They are so long that the humpback is sometimes called the winged whale. It is tempting to refer to these

Because of the position and shape of the blowholes in different species, it is often possible to identify a species of whale from several miles away by the shape and size of its blow.

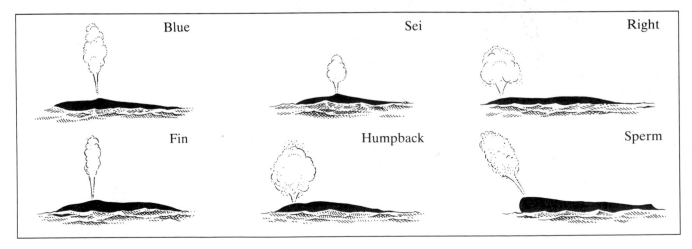

Blue
Sei
Right
Fin
Humpback
Sperm

appendages as fins, but they are, of course, modified forelimbs, a legacy of the whale's earlier existence on land.

Limbs are not the only inheritance from that former terrestrial life. At first a whale embryo has nostrils at the tip of its snout. By the time the foetus has grown to 1 in (2.54 cm) these have moved to the top of the head where they become blowholes. The baleen whales have two holes, and the toothed whales one. The sea-change experienced by the whale produced other problems which evolution has had to solve. A *Cetacean* has no hair to keep its warm-blooded body warm. Evolution's answer was a thick layer of fat or blubber. In right whales, during seasons of good feeding, this blubber can be as much as 2 ft (0.6 m) thick.

Sea life has conferred on the whale the gift of size. No land animal as big as one of the great whales could possibly exist. A stranded whale is doomed because the immense weight of its body can no longer be supported without the aid of water. It collapses, crushing the lungs so that it is no longer able to breath.

Humpbacks are known either as the singing whales or the winged whales. Their scientific name Megaptera novae-angliae. *'Megaptera' means giant-winged, a name that seems especially appropriate in this shot of a humpback breaching. Its winglike flippers are far longer than those of any other species.*

A humpback blows off the coast of Alaska. Whale expert Roger Payne believes that much of the water vapour in the blow comes from the sea water lying in the trough around the blowholes.

Whereas fish take in oxygen dissolved in water by means of gills, whales breath air like any other mammal. A whale can exhale and inhale within two to three seconds. It has been estimated that the air leaves the blowhole at around 300 mph. Since whales can stay submerged for 20 or 30 minutes, sometimes longer, it might be thought that their lungs are also enormous. Not so – the lung capacity is proportionately no larger than that of any land mammal. In the case of rorquals and sperm whales (the latter being the deepest divers of all) the lungs are proportionately smaller. Part of the secret is that the lightning-fast intake of breath replaces up to 90 per cent of the air in the lungs, whereas we can only change one tenth of our air. The whale's oxygen reserve is also far more efficiently distributed. Nearly half of it is stored in the muscles, about the same amount in the blood, with only 9 per cent in the tissues and 9 per cent in the lungs.

Most of the mammals that forsook the land for the sea return to the shore to breed. Whales mate, give birth and suckle at sea. The latter might be thought to cause serious problems for the whale calf, with the exceptionally rich milk being lost in the water before reaching the baby's mouth. To avoid this problem the mother whale ejects the milk with considerable force, shooting it directly into her calf's throat.

All these abilities are possessed by the humpback, but it has other talents that make it especially fascinating. Its amazing range of vocalization means it is also known as the singing whale.

The leading experts on the song of the humpback whale are the American scientists Roger and Katy Payne. They began their

America's leading woman marine biologist Dr Sylvia Earle records humpbacks bubble-netting in Glacier Bay with Chuck Juracz and his family aboard his research boat Jinjur.

sung each year. At a glance the overlap of theme from one year to the next was immediately clear.

They found, too, that though each whale sings its own version of the current theme, the song changes gradually, but with each singer using the same structure. It is as if the whales use the sonnet form one year, the ode the next year, Katy Payne suggests.

A spectograph electronically recorded a quartet of singing whales. This revealed that though all four were singing the same song, each singer appeared to be ignoring the other three. In effect there were four different versions, in four different tempos, and four different keys. Yet to record and analyse the songs is one thing, to understand their purpose and meaning another. Roger Payne is almost certain that the song is part of a breeding ritual since it occurs at no other time of the year, and it is only the males who sing it while remaining motionless in the water.

The bass notes that divers reported as having the force of a physical blow, are probably used for communicating over long distances, up to 50 miles (80 m). Roger Payne has suggested that before the day of the propeller-driven ship it may have been possible for any whale in any ocean to communicate with any other whales, no matter how far away. Today, the constant loud beat of many thousands of ships' propellers has made this impossible.

Jim Darling, of the West Coast Whale Research Foundation in Vancouver, has additional views. Song, he believes, may be the equivalent of a stag's antlers, being a display mechanism to establish dominance in the hierarchy. However, there the resemblance ends. Stags use their antlers to fight with rivals, while humpbacks usually settle their differences peacefully, the less dominant male sizing up his opponent by his song, and if outsung quietly swimming away. Only if two singers are evenly matched are they likely to come to blows, which can be quite violent, the huge tail flukes producing bloody wounds. Darling also suggests that more dominant animals establish their status with more complex tunes – hence the annual change of song.

Perhaps the final mystery is how humpbacks lacking vocal chords produce this varied repertoire of weird and impressive sounds. The most likely explanation suggests the use of valves and sacs in the whale's larynx.

Analysis of the songs exploded one scientific theory that had until then been taken for granted. It had been assumed that whales from one summer breeding ground stayed as a tight-knit community and migrated in winter to their northern feeding areas. Thus the whales from Maui wintered every year off the Aleutians. Those from Baja California wintered off southern Alaska. However, when Roger Payne listened to recordings of humpbacks singing in Mexico's Sea of Cortez, off the peninsular of Baja California he recognised passages of song that were peculiar to the humpbacks of Hawaii. It had been supposed that the two groups never mixed, yet further investigation, including taking close-up photographs of whales' tails by which humpbacks can be individually recognised, proved without doubt that humpbacks do not stay in tight little groups, as previously supposed. Instead, they range widely about the oceans, mixing stocks, so genetically benefiting the species.

Soon after filming and recording the humpbacks off Maui, Al Giddings and Sylvia Earle went north to Alaska to observe their winter feeding habits. By rights these should have been the humpbacks who summered off Baja California though it is now clear that this need not necessarily have been the case. For the record, however, none of the humpbacks they observed feeding in Glacier Bay, their Alaskan location, was known to them from Maui.

At this point it should perhaps be more fully explained that humpback whales have large areas of white on the underside of their flippers and more especially their tail flukes. These white markings are as individual as fingerprints. Moreover, the humpback is an aquabatic whale that seems to delight in breaching (leaping), showing its tail when it dives. Over a study period it is quite easy to build up a dossier of tail shots. The white markings, together with the shape of the trailing edge and tears in the flukes, make an individual whale easily identifiable.

Humpbacks do not feed on their breeding grounds. All their feeding is done in the cold northern waters when krill is most abundant. Every winter up to 20 humpbacks enter the remarkable Alaskan inlet called Glacier Bay. This 50 mile (80 m) long bay is where 12 glaciers drop their ice into the sea at the end of a long, slow journey from the coastal ranges.

Scientists studying the hump-back whale can easily identify individuals by the white markings on the underside of their tail flukes. Each pattern is as unique to the whale as are fingerprints to a human being.

31

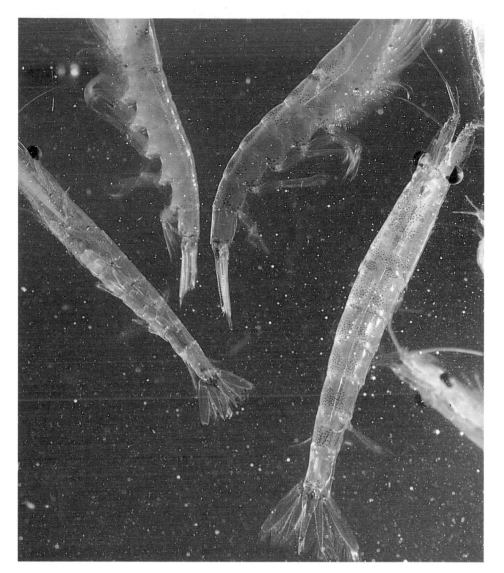

Facing page: Grey whales are ideal subjects for whale-watching by tourists as they migrate from the Arctic to Mexico close inshore. To human eyes they are possibly the least lovely of the whales, having a rather dirty grey and warty appearance with a row of knobs down their dorsal surface instead of a fin.

Krill is the Norwegian word for whale food. There are 13 species of these shrimplike creatures. The largest Euphausia superba is found in Antarctic waters. A single specimen weighs a tenth of a gramme yet it is likely that the total weight of krill in the Antarctic Ocean outweighs that of the entire human race.

Much of the whale study in Glacier Bay is carried out by Chuck Jurasz and his team, aboard the small motor vessel *Ginjur*. When the whales first arrive in the bay they are extremely active. It is possible they are just reacting to their new surroundings but their breachings and rollings do look joyfully playful. Humpbacks have a reputation for showing off in this way, each year attracting more and more tourist ships to the bay. Unfortunately, it has been reported that the whales often react with a violent movement when a ship passes. The National Parks Service, responsible for Glacier Bay, view that increasing boat traffic with some concern, afraid it might adversely affect the whales.

What the tourists on the cruise ships never see, however, is the activity for which the whales come to the bay.

Whales are at the top of a very short food chain. Solar energy produces phyto- or vegetable plankton. Krill eat plankton and whales eat krill. The species of krill in Glacier Bay is much smaller than the euphausids in the Antarctic. The whales, however, are more than satisfied with this diet, often feeding for 18 hours a day.

The humpbacks (one of the most efficient converters of energy into flesh and bone) mainly use three methods of harvesting krill in Glacier Bay. The first has been named 'lunge-feeding'. With this technique the whale detects a concentration of krill, then opens its mouth and accelerates horizontally through it. This is probably a variation, used in enclosed waters, of the mass scooping up of food practised when cruising slowly in the open ocean. From time to time, a pair of whales combine to lunge-feed together. Sometimes a whale lunges on its side or even on its back. In the later case, the great weight of water taken on board helps to close the mouth. As it takes in hundreds of gallons of water with its meal, the pleats on the underside of the whale's jaw ripple and distend like a collapsing tyre. They enable the mouth to expand to accommodate such huge quantities of water.

The second method is 'flick feeding'. The tail fluke is thrown violently forward, impelling the krill swarms towards the cavernous mouth. The whales' large tongue helps compress the catch against the baleen plates, which filter out the food.

The third method is even more astonishing. It was first observed off Greenland in 1928, but no one believed the reports. When it happened in Glacier Bay, Chuck Jurasz and Roger Payne were there to unravel its mysteries. It is known as 'bubble-netting'. The process starts with a ring of very large, almost football-sized bubbles and ends with the whale surfacing nearly vertically, with its mouth wide open, in the centre of the bubble ring. The whale closes its mouth taking in a huge quantity of water and krill. The whole technique is designed to concentrate as much krill as possible in the middle of the net of bubbles. While the bubbles are being blown the whale makes a noise like a steam engine starting to pull a train out of a station.

A humpback lunge-feeding by ploughing horizontally through a concentration of krill with its mouth open. The pinkish tongue can be seen quite clearly. When the whale closes its mouth, baleen plates in the throat will filter out the krill from hundreds of gallons of water which are then ejected.

When a whale has spotted a dense mass of krill, it begins its manoeuvre deep down. The humpback swims round in a tight circle as it begins to blow the bubbles, spiralling upwards towards the surface. In this way the first bubbles reach the surface about the same time as the whale is blowing the last of them. The thunderous noise, together with the rising circle of bubbles, drives the mass of krill together into the centre of the ring. On its last turn, the whale straightens up and rises vertically. All the humpback needs to do is open its mouth, and take in the catch floating in the water. At this point, the pleats under the jaw are fully distended. The water is squeezed out, but the krill remain trapped by the baleen plates.

There is a pleasing postscript to the story of the humpback whale. When the spaceship *Voyager* was launched on an incredible journey which would take it thousands of years away from earth, it carried with it tapes of the most evocative sounds of this planet. One of them was the song of the humpback whale. *Voyager* has now passed out of our solar system into the black void of outer space. It seems sadly typical of modern man that he should be clever enough to launch the song of the humpback among the stars, but insensitive enough to kill the singer of that song here upon his own planet.

A unique shot of a humpback bubble-netting. The circle of bubbles that concentrates the krill has reached the surface and the bubbles have burst. The whale has probably already scooped up the krill in the centre of the bubbles and is preparing to dive.

Stranded on South Georgia

The island of South Georgia is about 120 miles (193 km), snowfields and glaciers. The only habitations are the scientific bases of the British Antarctic Survey an the two derelict whaling stations at Grytviken and Leith. The Falkland Islands lie 400 miles (644 km) off the coast of Argentina and South Georgia is a further 800 miles (1,287 km) south-east. As it lies outside the Antarctic Circle the climate is much less severe than on the Antarctic continent. Nevertheless, this is a desolate, if beautiful place.

Initially, there seems to be little of interest here. As far as is known there are no rich mineral deposits locked away in the rocks, and no offshore oil. Yet, almost from the moment the island was put on the map, people have been sailing south to exploit its natural riches, to some degree changing its environment, and recently even fighting over it. South Georgia is a perfect illustration of just how far people will travel to make a profit.

The first sightings of the island were, as is often the case, accidental. The discoverers had been blown off course in the stormy Southern Ocean. The first arrival was again apparently accidental. It is thought to have involved a London merchant, Antoine de la Roche. His ship was blown south from around Cape Horn, at the southern tip of South America, ending up at an anchorage at the south end of South Georgia. That was in 1675. Eighty one years later, the 486 tonne ship *Leon* was blown east from Cape Horn and sighted the island, returning with stories of penguins and great numbers of whales.

The tales of these accidental discoveries reawoke beliefs popular since Elizabethan times suggesting that in the far Southern Ocean

A well-grown king penguin chick begs for food. For the moment, the parent is more concerned with calling, perhaps to its partner or maybe to warn intruders away.

South Georgia lies outside the Arctic Circle and enjoys a fairly mild climate, at least when compared with Antarctica itself. Inland, away from the sea, it is a forbidding but beautiful island of mountain ranges and glaciers.

lay a land rich in gems and minerals. In 1772, two expeditions were sent south by Britain and France. One, led by Yves de Kerguelen, who has a sub-antarctic island named after him, returned with glowing but unfounded reports. The other expedition came nearer the truth when it christened such land as it had visited the 'Land of Desolation'. It was left to the greatest sailor–explorer of all, Captain James Cook, to put South Georgia officially on the map for Britain.

In 1772 he sailed south with two naval sloops – *HMS Resolution* of 462 tonnes, and *HMS Adventure*, 336 tonnes. He tried to break through the pack ice to reach the great continent which he believed, correctly, to lie to the south. He was the first navigator to pass south of the Antarctic Circle, but the ice beat him and he never sighted Antarctica, or *Terra Australis*, as it was then named. However, in January 1775 he landed on South Georgia and claimed it for Britain. He left two place names behind him: Possession Bay, where he had landed to annex the island; and Cape Disappointment, the southern tip of South Georgia, the point at which he realised this was an island and not a part of the great southern continent.

Cook's description was not one calculated to make fleets of adventurers rush south. He described South Georgia and the South

Sandwich Islands to its east as: 'Lands doomed by Nature to perpetual frigidness: never to feel the warmth of the sun's rays; whose savage aspects I have not words to describe.' In one respect, however, Cook's accounts did excite the murderous and greedy. He described in detail the great numbers of seals and whales he had sighted.

The destruction of the world's seal colonies in the latter half of the nineteenth and first years of the twentieth century ranks in terms of mass slaughter with the near extermination of the American bison, and the present killing of the African elephant. The freezing weather and stormy seas did not deter the American and British sealers, provided there were new areas to be exploited. The sealers approached South Georgia in 1784. By 1830 the island's millions of fur and elephant seals had virtually become extinct. The slaughter was indiscriminate. Age or sex made no difference. Fur seals were killed for their valuable skins with blows to the head. Elephant seals were killed to satisfy the large market for seal oil.

It has been estimated that 2–3 million fur seals were killed, and about ¾ million elephant seals. Fortunately, seal oil became less important with the discovery of petroleum, and the last sealers came to South Georgia in 1912. In 1909 The Seal Fishery

Three adult king penguins prepare to set off on a fishing trip that may take them two or three weeks to catch the food they need for their growing young.

39

A mature bull elephant seal can reach 18 ft in length and weigh nearly three tonnes. The size of the male's nose largely dictates its status in the sexual hierarchy and plays a part in deciding who will get the largest number of females. Despite their bulk, the bulls can move surprisingly quickly. Cindy Buxton approaches this one with proper care.

Ordinance had set commercial quotas for elephant seals, and gave fur seals all over the world complete protection. Being remarkably resilient creatures their numbers built up again very quickly. The fur and elephant seal populations of South Georgia are today probably as high as they have ever been.

Yet sealers were not the only problem. Whales were slaughtered in the Southern Ocean, largely because of the bases on South Georgia, though whaling stations were set up on other islands too. Today, great piles of whale bones and rusting vats, huts and machinery are all that remain of the whaling industry that wiped out the great whales in the Antarctic seas. There is one exception to this sad decline, the minke whale, a small rorqual, whose population in the Southern Ocean is now said to be ½ million by Dr Richard Laws, Director of the British Antarctic Survey.

The whalers and sealers did secondary damage to the virgin island they had invaded. Inevitably rats escaped from their ships – brown rats, in the case of South Georgia (ship's rats are usually the black species). They exterminated at least one indigenous bird on the main island, the South George pipit. Other changes occurred from 1911–1925 when the whalers introduced three herds of reindeer to provide fresh meat, as there are no indigenous land mammals in sub-Antarctica or on the Antarctic continent. Two of these introductions flourished. The reindeer population now varies between 400–800, enough to inflict serious damage on the fragile indigenous plant life, notably the lichens. Apart from the vegetation, it is probably fair to conclude that South Georgia has not been greatly scarred by mankind's worst efforts. Alas, the same cannot be said with any confidence about the surrounding seas which support its natural life.

The cold southern waters are extremely rich in food supplies for seals and seabirds. Fish, jellyfish and squid abound. But the most incredible concentration of food is represented by the shrimplike

Between 1911 and 1925, three groups of reindeer were introduced to South Georgia by the whalers whose derelict station can be seen in the background. They proved disastrous to the native environment, doing considerable damage to the sparse indigenous vegetation. The reindeer now number several thousand.

creatures known collectively as krill, a Norwegian word meaning whale food. There are 19 species of this crustacean, the largest of which is *Euphausia superba*, a creature about 2½ in (6–7 cm) long. Krill form the largest single biomass on earth. There are probably 600,000 billion of them. They weigh more than the entire human race (you would need over 650 million tonnes of people to outbalance them). Krill exist in both cold northern and southern waters, but the biggest concentrations are around Antarctica.

The impact of the whalers on the Southern Ocean has meant that, now the great whales have been greatly reduced in numbers, there is more krill for other species. With such prevaling overabundance it might seem that this fact would make little difference, but penguins and other seabirds are undoubtedly benefiting. Adelie, chinstrap and macaroni penguins have all shown marked increases in numbers. Birds and other krill-eaters probably account for 115 million tonnes of krill each year. There is, however, one big problem which affects the wildlife not only on the Antarctic mainland, but also on islands such as South Georgia. Since 1960 the USSR has been harvesting krill, detecting the dense swarms with an echo-sounder, and sweeping them up using trawls with an entrance 656 ft (200 m) square. Since 1960, at least 3 million tonnes of krill have been harvested. At first there were difficulties in processing and freezing the catch, which were subsequently overcome. Now there is a marketing problem. But if krill products can be successfully marketed to the public, especially in Japan, then krill fishing could become an enormous industry with a serious effect on the ocean's eco-system and tragic results for the seabird colonies.

Giant petrels are the universal scavengers of the Sub-Antarctic islands. They also prey upon eggs and chicks. Here, like vultures, they dispose of a seal carcass and, like scavenging vultures, they are red around the neck with blood.

The fishing industry has already made great inroads on the fish stocks around South Georgia. The whalers knew that there were vast quantities of the South Georgia cod on the island's shallow shelf, but they were after bigger game. In 1960, the USSR opened up this fishery and by 1970 was catching 400,000 tonnes a year, after which, not surprisingly, fish stocks sharply declined.

The lesson is familiar and urgent. Remote and apparently impregnable places such as South Georgia – and even more so the Antarctic – are very fragile. It is a lesson we never learn, particularly when ecological well-being depends not so much on the land but on the surrounding seas.

South Georgia and its smaller islands, notably Bird Island to the north, are home to hundreds of thousands of breeding seabirds – petrels, penguins, skuas, shags, gulls, terns, and one of the most beautiful of the albatrosses, the light-mantled sooty albatross. But the most striking bird colony of all is to be found at St Andrews Bay, 10 hazardous miles (16 km) across mountains and glaciers from Grytviken, but only two hours by sea.

In October 1981 Cindy Buxton and Annie Price – two young wildlife film-makers – were landed by the British Antarctic Survey

A macaroni penguin feeds its chick. It closely resembles the rockhopper penguin except that it is slightly bigger and has a gold patch in the centre of its forehead between the plumes. Rockhoppers seem quite content to let macaronis nest in their colonies.

43

Like emperor penguins, kings brood their single egg on their feet, lowering an abdominal fold to cover it. This parent is tucking the egg in after taking over nesting duties from its partner.

ship *Bransfield*, at St Andrews Bay, to spend the summer making a film about the 10,000 strong king penguin colony. They had a small wooden hut, just big enough to cook and sleep in (previously erected by the Survey for their own observers), a radio, solar panels to charge their batteries, and enough rations to last them until the relief ship returned the following April. Before their self-imposed exile was over, they were to make world headlines. Yet their only aim was to make the first-ever complete record of the king penguin's unusual breeding behaviour.

The king penguin is a large and remarkably handsome bird. The adults have a dark orange bib on their chests, and a yellow stripe up each side of the head, with a matching yellowish-orange lower mandible, or beak. The king penguin is second in size and magnificence only to the emperor penguin, which breeds on the sea ice of the Antarctic mainland during the bitter and total night of mid-winter.

The emperor lays its egg in late summer. The egg is placed on top of the feet and the lower abdomen drops like a brood pouch to protect it. Hatching takes 65 days. Afterwards, the chicks are brooded for a further 40 days. All this happens in temperatures of up to −50°C (−32°F) or worse, and winds that often reach more than 100mph. The emperor is equipped to withstand 10 degrees more cold than the king penguin. Its greater size protects it to some extent from heat loss, though flippers, feet and nasal passages have complex systems to defeat the intense cold.

The main secret of its survival is togetherness. The phenomenon is aptly known as huddling, with as many as 5,000 kings packed together, 10 birds per 1–2 yd^2 (1 sq m). To avoid birds being exposed to the terrible wind-chill for too long, the windward birds continually waddle down the colony – with an egg balanced on their feet – and rejoin the queue from the downwind or sheltered side. As a result the whole nesting colony moves slowly into the wind, thus reducing total heat loss by up to 50 per cent.

The king penguin has a much more complicated breeding system. The eggs are laid in early December. On South Georgia this is the start of the summer. The large, fluffy-coated brown young are fledged and reach 90 per cent of their adult weight by June, when winter sets in. During the winter months food is hard to obtain, but the parents usually find supplies at sea, returning to feed their young every two or three weeks. If the parents cannot find food easily, the young birds may have to fast for two or three months.

The following spring the parents start vigorously feeding their young on squid, often caught 30 miles (48 km) offshore. They continue doing so until the chicks are ready to go to sea during November and December. Yet before the adults can breed again, they must moult. They could not afford to do this while catching food for their young, so this essential process of renewing plumage waits until now. The penguins breed again in March, when they

King penguin courtship rituals are stately and usually courteous. They include 'head-flagging', when the head is waved from side to side to show off the yellow patches.

usually produce a far smaller chick. A good many of these die in the coming winter. Because of this somewhat complicated system, king penguins can only average two births every three years.

King penguin courtship rituals are delightfully stately. Ornithologists have terms to describe every behavioural gesture. There is head-flagging – which makes the most of the brilliant orange auricular patches; and the attraction walk – usually performed by the male. In the early stages of courtship, a pair will often wander together for two or three days before finding a suitable site. Kings do not make a nest but simply command a breeding territory 2–3 ft (0.76 m) in diameter. Anyone who ventures too close is made

Mutual preening occurs at a fairly advanced state of court-ship, usually when the nest site has been chosen.

This pair has settled down at a nest site. No real nest is actually made. Mating will now take place within two or three days.

47

The Union Jack was presented to Cindy Buxton before leaving for South Georgia by the landlord of her local pub in Norfolk. Cindy and Annie hoisted it when they heard the Argentines had invaded but later prudently hauled it down in case they were spotted from the air. They flew it again as soon as they heard that the Royal Marines had recaptured Grytviken.

extremely unwelcome. When the single egg is laid, the birds roll it onto their feet, just like their larger relatives the emperor penguins, and cover it with an abdominal fold.

Initially, the female broods the egg for the first few hours, then alternates with her mate for a day or two. After that he takes over for the next two or three weeks while she goes on a deep-sea fishing expedition. The change-over is always an anxious time. Skuas and sheathbills, scavengers of the nesting colonies, snap up any eggs that are not well guarded.

Most birds will only feed their own chicks. King penguins are an exception. For the first week or so of its life, an orphan or even a temporarily deserted chick becomes a colony responsibility with any bird brooding or feeding it. But this only applies for the first week. After that the young become identifiable by their individual feeding calls. They also recognise the calls of their parents.

Cindy Buxton and Annie Price, who filmed these behavioural patterns for *Survival*, had completed most of their project by April 1982, after six month's work. Every day at a set time they phoned the British Antarctic Survey base, at Grytviken, to give a progress check. But on April 3, 1982, their radio link with Grytviken was cut. The Argentines had invaded South Georgia, the first move in their ill-fated attempt to capture South Georgia and the Falkland Islands. Though their radio link with Grytviken had gone, the two girls heard on the wireless that South Georgia had been invaded and Grytviken taken. Their reply, in true blue British fashion, was to run up the Union Jack on an improvised mast and carry on filming, so risking capture. Later, three Antarctic Survey scientists hiked overland from Grytviken to join them. On April 25 they heard distant rumblings which they thought were made by glaciers. It was, in fact, the Royal Navy retaking the base at Grytviken. Soon after they were rescued.

The Argentine impact on the landscape and wildlife was negligible, a few shell and mortar craters, and scrap-iron in the form of a wrecked submarine and a downed helicopter, both of which could be removed. But the larger implications remain. Why did Argentina invade? Certainly for territorial reasons. But why did they try to capture South Georgia as well as the Falklands? Argentina clearly had her sights set firmly on Antarctica. Their 'scientific' base, Esperanza, at the northernmost tip of the Antarctic peninsular, now appears to have been at least part military. Argentina even sent a pregnant woman there too give birth to 'the first citizen of Antarctica.'

The present international treaty governing the shared responsibility for the non-military use of, and non-exploitation of Antarctica comes up for review in 1991. Will Antarctica then be 'up for grabs'? If it seems a pity to cast a political shadow over this remarkable area, rich in natural treasures, it is unavoidable and even necessary. Much depends on how the Southern Ocean is governed and harvested in the future.

Survival and *Endurance*

At the start of the First World War, South Georgia became the starting and finishing point of one of the most heroic journeys ever made in polar regions. In December, 1914, the little wooden ship *Endurance* sailed from South Georgia carrying an expedition of 27, led by Ernest Shackleton. His objective was to land on the Antarctic mainland and become the first person to cross it.

Almost at once the ship hit abnormal ice conditions. Sometimes she was stuck fast, all hands having to climb over the side with giant saws to cut the boat free. Excellent photographs were taken of the early part of this voyage by the expedition's photographer, Frank Hurley. Despite the appalling ice conditions, Shackleton drove the expedition south. *Endurance* was built to survive the worst conditions of pack ice

and he was confident it would survive. However, once the boat had edged her way into the Weddell Sea she hit deep trouble. A freak storm had driven the ice up against the mainland. The pack ice was stuck and so, six weeks after setting sail, was the *Endurance*. By the end of February it was certain the ship had no chance of breaking free for at least another nine months.

At first there was plenty to be done, seals to be killed and their flesh frozen for dog food. Also, dog teams were trained in case they were needed for a break-out. Frank Hurley filmed all this, including the crew playing football on the ice. Then the long winter night set in and the crew lived in perpetual darkness. Yet just when spring should have set them

A king penguin colony. Numbers rise to nearly 50,000 birds at breeding time

free, the crew heard a terrible booming. The ice grip was getting tighter. The *Endurance* was the strongest wooden ship ever built. In places her walls were 3 ft (9 m) thick. The ice cracked her open like a rotten walnut.

Shackleton was still not defeated. He planned to sit tight on the ice, in what he christened 'Ocean Camp', and let the ice carry them north-west towards land. He knew his major problems would begin when the ice began to relax its grip, and they took to the boats. At one point he even decided to sledge the boats across the ice towards land, but the going was dreadful. After 6 miles (9.6 km) they had to give up.

At last, six months after they had abandoned ship, the ice on which they had camped began to crack. They launched the three ship's boats in a murderous sea of grinding ice floes. After five stormy days, they sighted a wind-torn lump of rock called Elephant Island. No one had previously landed here; not even the sealers visited this desolate place. Shackleton got his boats ashore in a small cove where there was very little protection from the sea. Very soon it became clear that someone had to go for help. Naturally that someone was Shackleton. They fitted out the most seaworthy of the three small boats, the *James Caird*, decking it as far as possible with canvas. The only hope was to reach South Georgia, 800 miles (1,287 km) away across one of the stormiest seas in the world. Shackleton set sail with five companions, leaving the rest of the crew on that freezing beach to feed on penguins and whatever else they could find. They did not expect to see Shackleton again.

Thanks to the superb navigation by Frank Worsley, skipper of the *Endurance*, they sighted South Georgia after 17 appalling days. But their troubles were by no means over. They had landed on the south side of the island at King Haakon Bay. The nearest help was at Stromness, whence they had originally sailed, which lay across South Georgia's massive range of mountains.

Shackleton took two men with him, Worsley and the second officer of the *Endurance*, Tom Crean. He judged the other three not fit enough for the ordeal that lay ahead, and told them to stay on the shore. He would return for them. Again, the odds against this happening seemed enormous, but I suspect that these three had such faith in Shackleton that they never doubted that he would make it.

To cross those mountains is a feat by any standards, even when properly equipped. Shackleton had no idea of the route, the conditions or the difficulties. His equipment consisted of just a length of rope, an adze, a small cooking stove, and a pot.

They made time-wasting and exhausting mistakes.

Ernest Shackleton's grave at Grytviken.

At one point the only way to descend a steep ice slope was to sit on a coil of rope, push off, and hope for the best. But luck at last shone on Shackleton. The South Georgia weather is notoriously unreliable. By some miracle there were three continuous fine days during the mountain crossing, otherwise they would never have made it.

When the party eventually walked into the whaling station, the resident Norwegian whalers ran in terror from these wild, blackened men who had crossed mountains no one had crossed before.

Shackleton sailed the next day to pick up the three men left at King Haakon Bay. He had to wait four months for the ice to break up sufficiently before he could set out in a Chilean ice-breaker to rescue the 22 men still on Elephant Island. Amazingly, they were all alive. Shackleton had not lost a single man. Tragically, one of the survivors joined the navy and was killed at the Battle of Jutland. Shackleton returned to South Georgia after the war and died there. He is buried at Grytviken.

Krakatoa – The Day That Shook The World

In May 1883, a dormant volcano on a remote island in the Sunda Strait, between Java and Sumatra, began a series of violent eruptions. It belched out vast clouds of ash that obscured the sun. The explosions were heard 70 miles (112 km) away. By the end of May the 'fireworks' were dying down, though ships passing through the straits at night could still see the reflected glow of molten lava in the crater.

In mid-June, large-scale eruptions began again and tremors were felt in parts of Java and Sumatra. Although the crater formed by the first explosions had been blown away, there were now at least 10 more craters. They hurled out steam and pumice dust to such a height that ash fell on villages up to 300 miles (483 km) away.

The climax came on 27 August 1883, with an explosion calculated to have been equal to 3,000 atomic bombs. The island of Krakatoa disappeared with a bang that was heard as far away as Australia and Ceylon. It was the loudest noise the world had ever known. Surprisingly, the actual explosion killed very few people, but the havoc was caused by the seismic tidal waves, called tsunamis, that followed. Some were over 100 ft (30 m) high.

The tsunamis swept through low-lying areas, wiping out mainland towns and villages, including the small port of Anger. It is estimated that 30,000 people were drowned. Contemporary engravings depict ships sailing through seas of corpses, while photographs show scenes reminiscent of the aftermath of Hiroshima. The giant waves had flattened everything, including a hotel and a fort. A Dutch gunboat struck by 90 ft (27 m) waves was picked up and hurled over 1 mile (1.6 km) into the jungle.

Anak Krakatoa, 'Son of Krakatoa', blows its top in a recent violent eruption. In 1928, this new volcano emerged from the seabed ominously close to the place where Krakatoa itself exploded in 1883.

After the 'big bang', there was one more minor explosion and then silence. The dust rose 50 miles (80 km) high, circling the earth and causing spectacular sunsets for years afterwards. Half the island of Krakatoa had disappeared, much of it blown into the upper atmosphere.

The main island had been over 7 miles (11 km) long. Today, only fragments remain, the largest being Rakata. The smaller island of the group actually increased in size due to the huge deposits of volcanic ash that fell on it. Between these islands is now a new volcano, already 1,000 ft (305 m) high. It emerged from the seabed in 1928, ominously close to the point at which the 1883 eruptions began. From the sea nearby rise a group of shattered rocks like jagged fangs. These teeth protrude from the broken jaw of Krakatoa's old crater. Below is the empty magma chamber, into which the sea rushed to become super-heated steam, and into which most of the old Krakatoa collapsed, causing the big final explosion.

The new volcano (called Anak Krakatoa – son of Krakatoa) is growing fast. Unfortunately seismologists cannot predict whether this young volcano will one day give a repeat performance.

This is by no means the only volcano in Indonesia. It boasts more than 1,000. In 1982 I visited Krakatoa to film it. The night before setting out in a local shark-fishing boat, the only means of transport available, Anak Krakatoa made its presence felt. Though still nearly 100 miles (160 km) from our camp on the mainland, the eruptions sounded and looked like a tremendous electrical storm far below the seaward horizon. Indeed, I thought that such a storm was the cause of the distant flashes. When I learned that the son of Krakatoa was in fact responsible, I knew how it must have felt to look across the Sunda Strait 100 years before. In fact, Anak Krakatoa was behaving like a perfectly normal young volcano. Later it even attempted to demolish our cameraman's tent by rolling a rock the size of a small truck narrowly past in the middle of the night. In a second near lethal incident, earlier in the year, dust from another of Indonesia's volcanoes, Galanggung, blocked the engines of a Boeing 747 at 33,000 ft (10 km), though mercifully the captain was able to restart them.

The reason why the area is so rich in volcanoes is that it lies close to the edge of the Australian Plate, one of the moving plates on which the continents, and the oceans, sit. The theory of Plate Tectonics is recent, critical clues being discovered only in the 1950s. In the following two decades many scientists, mainly from the USA, Canada, France and Britain, added solid evidence to what at the outset had been an intriguing theory without much scientific support.

The theory, crudely described, is as follows. Look at the outlines of Africa and South America and you can imagine them just fitting together like pieces of a rather poorly made jigsaw. How, then, did they move apart? As early as 1912 the German scientist Alfred

Wegener had advanced a theory that the continents and oceans had drifted apart some 200 million years ago, after the break-up of what was once one huge landmass called Panagea, or All Earth. He backed up his theory with evidence of similar fossils found in Africa, South America, and India. In the 1920s, Wegener's theory was virtually forgotten and even openly discredited.

However, in the 1950s evidence began to gather, revealing that the magnetism in the rocks of various continents showed that they had moved in relation to the North Pole. Wegener argued that the continents sailed through the rock of the upper mantle. He was, as the new discoveries showed, on the right lines but wrong in detail. The scientists who were assembling the theory of Plate Tectonics agreed that the continents were actually embedded in the thick plates of the lithosphere, but were moving apart as Wegener had proposed. An astonishing programme of research with submersibles – small submarines capable of operating as much as 1.8 miles (3 km) below the surface – began to map the ocean floor. Project FAMOUS (The French–American Mid-Ocean Ridge Undersea Study) discovered evidence – in the form of lava – that backed the theory of ocean floors spreading and cracking in a series of deep valleys and faults, with molten rock welling up where these faults occurred.

Marine life is gradually re-establishing itself around the base of Anak Krakatoa. A large clam lies partially buried in volcanic ash. Deposits of ash from frequent eruptions make life hard for the formation of corals.

In the 1960s an even more ambitious programme was launched. The specially built, deep-sea drilling ship *Global Challenger* drilled 400 holes during 44 cruises. Core samples of rock and sediment were taken from the ocean bed, further confirming the theory of Continental Drift. These cores clearly showed which land masses had been adjacent to each other in far distant times, and how the oceans had spread.

But how do these theories relate to Krakatoa? The answer is as follows. Where plates meet, or separate, cracks occur through which the molten heart of the earth is liable to well up and escape. Sometimes the lava gushes out in floes similar to those emitted by surface volcanoes. At others the molten lava cools on contact with the cold sea water, the suddenly hardening outer skin breaking to allow more lava to gush out. The resulting rounded boulders are known as pillow lava. On a grander scale, undersea volcanoes grow and grow until they reach the surface, often forming complete islands. The Hawaiian chain is one famous example, as are the islands of the Galapagos archipelago. However, Krakatoa will probably remain the most famous of all volcanoes that started life on the sea bed because of its hugely dramatic eruption in December 1883.

Recently formed volcanic islands are fascinating to scientists because they begin at zero as habitats for plant and animal life. Recent lava and volcanic ash is extremely inhospitable. Only after many years will it become sufficiently weathered and broken down to form soil with sufficient nutrients to support plant growth. In this respect, Anak Krakatoa and Rakata, the largest surviving chunk of the original island, are living laboratories.

Facing page: Two days after cameraman Dieter Plage climbed to the top of Anak Krakatoa to take this picture, the volcano produced a major eruption. Sulphur and ash from previous eruptions lie around the crater rim. In the distance is the island of Rakata, the largest surviving part of the original Krakatoa.

Life on Anak Krakatoa is so far confined to the eastern tip. Prevailing winds carry much of the ash away from this area so that vegetation has a chance to establish itself. Seeds borne on the wind and carried by the sea have, in 60 years, created a small woodland there.

Water monitor lizards are likely to be one of the first reptile colonists of Anak Krakatoa. It lies only 25 miles (40 km) from Ujong Kulon, no distance for such an accomplished swimmer. Monitors are opportunist feeders and will certainly find crabs along the shore of the new volcano.

Anak Krakatoa which has a surprisingly diverse flora, including barringtonias, pandanus and casuarina trees. The ground cover in this woodland consists of a variety of mosses, grasses, ferns and some flowering plants such as convolvulus.

But how does such a wide variety of plant and animal life arrive at offshore islands like these? The answer is that the ocean is like a great conveyor belt. The lighter seeds undoubtedly arrive by air, either in birds' plumage or borne on the wind, as were the spiders sailing on their gossamer parachutes. The majority of colonists, however, travel by sea.

The islands that were once Krakatoa are exceptionally well placed to receive such immigrants. The jungles of Ujong Kulon, which Krakatoa helped to form, are barely 25 miles (40 km) to the south and, with a prevailing wind and current for six months of the year, are ideally placed as 'delivery agents'.

Many of the larger seeds are buoyant and salt-water proof. A few arrive at Rakata, or even Anak Krakatoa, and even fewer succeed in getting a root-hold, but once achieved the results are spectacular.

Where trees and ground cover develop, there will soon be insects and arachnids, geckos which feed on them, and snakes to feed on the geckos. There may even be monitor lizards to prey on the snakes. Many reptiles are excellent swimmers, and 25 miles is not beyond the range of a current-carried python. When not swimming, a snake can float and, even in salt water, submerge for a very long time. However, it is more likely that the majority of the reptiles and insects and spiders rafted here on fallen and rotten trees, from the nearby jungles of Ujong Kulon. Birds can easily fly to offshore islands, but they will only stay when there is food for themselves and their young, and also nesting habitats. Provided the basics exist, birds will inventively adapt. Many kingfishers excavate their nests by tunnelling into banks. Since the volcanic ash on Rakata is too crumbly for this purpose, the few collared kingfishers that have settled on the island have found an alternative nesting site. They hack out tunnels in the cement-like substance from which the tree termites make their nests. Once settled the kingfishers benefit from the lack of competition for the supplies of small fish.

In one other habitat the vanished Krakatoa has given scientists a clean sheet to commence their research: the reefs off Krakatoa are amazingly rich in life. Here marine biologists can date the birth of the corals almost to the hour. The one element that the polyps which build a coral reef cannot abide is silt. Such reefs as were not completely destroyed by the great eruption were covered by up to 98 ft (30 m) of volcanic ash. Today, the 100-year-old reefs off Anak Krakatoa are as diverse in marine life as any in the tropical seas.

When the 50–100 ft (15–30 m) high tsunamis generated by Krakatoa's explosion swept across the Sunda Strait they flattened everything in their path, including the jungles of Ujong Kulon. Today these jungles are the last home of the Javan rhino. There are perhaps 50 of these animals left in the world, and all live here.

One of the rarest large mammals on earth – the Javan Rhino. It only exists in Ujong Kulon and probably would not survive at all had not Krakatoa's great explosion driven the people from those jungles, never to return.

Sadly, the tsunamis killed all the people living in the jungles too. To have survived, the rhinos and other large animals must have been on high ground at the time of the disaster, although some may have recolonised Ujong Kulon soon afterwards from other areas. However, since the human inhabitants never recolonised this part of the jungle, Ujong Kulon is now a national park with no human habitation inside its boundaries.

When you try to move through the jungle it is easy to see why even on Java, one of the world's most heavily populated islands where every inch of living space is at a premium, no one has tried to move back. The jungle is impenetrable. The only way to make any progress inside Ujong Kulon is by taking a dug-out canoe and paddling up one of the twisting, overgrown jungle rivers, such as the Cigenter.

On the grey mud banks where the little river meets the ocean, life is abundant. It is that kind of half-life, common to river mouths everywhere, in which the life-forms owe something to the land, and even more to the sea. On the mud, which still contains a good deal of ash from Krakatoa's explosion, there are skittering hordes of mudskippers, little fish that have not quite made up their minds whether to live on land or in the water. Every few minutes this pop-eyed little fish dips itself in the water to breath dissolved oxygen. It is pop-eyed because it has periscopic bifocal eyes. When alarmed it moves with a fast skating motion across the mud. The sudden appearance of a hungry monitor lizard reveals that it can skip equally fast across the surface of the water.

Mudskippers, members of the goby family of fishes, have not made up their minds whether to live on land or in water. They compromise by occupying the muddy banks of mangrove swamps and tropical estuaries. When on land they keep their respiratory chambers full of water so that they can breath dissolved oxygen. Their fins are 'elbowed' for walking across mud.

The mud flats of the Cigenter are also home to thousands of tiny, brightly coloured fiddler crabs. The male crabs are armed with one gigantic claw and one minute one. They seem to spend their entire time waving their big claw in a menacing fashion, the action which provides their name. This act is one of demonstration rather than naked aggression. Its function is to intimidate rivals in territorial squabbles. The very small claw is used for a more practical purpose – feeding. The drabber females have two small claws. The strange fact about these little crabs is that they are not all, so to speak, right-handed. Quite a large proportion have enlarged left claws, so that it is quite possible to find a left-clawed fiddler disputing a feeding ground with a right-clawed rival. Such disagreements resemble a bout between a normal boxer and a 'south paw'. When the tide flows, each crab cuts a disc of mud which it carries on its shell and holds in place with a claw. It seals the mouth of its burrow with this, trapping a bubble of air which it breathes until the tide recedes.

This brackish water world has its land-based predators, fish and crab-eating birds such as herons, and jungle and water monitor lizards. The deadliest predator of all, possibly one of the most lethal water predators in the world, hunts the Cigenter River and its mud banks. The estuarine or salt-water crocodile is aggressive even by the standards of its own kind. It can grow to 15 ft (4.5 m) in length, and has a considerably longer muzzle than the freshwater species of the Far East. In some parts of Indonesia estuarine crocodiles are thought to spend their entire lives in the sea, except

The mud banks of the Cigenter river are home to countless thousands of tiny fiddler crabs. Their name comes from the menacing-looking claw, carried only by the males, which is constantly moving like a fiddler's elbow. The claw is waved to stake out territory and warn off rivals.

for excursions ashore to lay eggs. They do, however, make quite long journeys overland and certainly lie in wait on mud banks for deer and wild pigs coming to drink. Even monkeys preoccupied with catching fiddler crabs quite frequently fall victim.

The Cigenter River is less than 5 miles (8 km) long. Much of its water is brakish and many of its fish are adapted to not-quite-salt, not-quite-fresh conditions. Though strictly speaking a freshwater fish, one of the inhabitants of Ujong Kulon's jungle streams deserves special mention. Insects abound among the jungle vegetation, where you might think they would be perfectly safe from fish, particularly when sitting on leaves and branches over 1 ft (0.3 m) above the surface. Yet they are far from safe from the archer fish, which shoots a drop of water at its victims. It does so by means of a groove in the upper part of its mouth which acts as a gun barrel. Pressure from its gills propels the water drop like a pellet. The archer fish shoots with superb accuracy and sufficient power to knock insects as big as grasshoppers into the river, where they can be eaten.

Although the dominant theme in this book is man's adverse effect on the oceans, it is interesting to note here how nature itself can, at times, dwarf even our malign influence. Yet Krakatoa did also yield many benefits. The volcano created both a unique sea and land wilderness containing rare and wonderful forms of life, which it is within our power to protect and preserve. Indonesia has shown its good intentions by turning Ujong Kulon into a national park. It will require considerable international support and help to maintain it.

The jungles of Ujong Kulon are so dense today that they might never have been wiped out by the 50 foot waves caused by Krakatoa's great eruption. Their lushness is the result of over one hundred inches of rain each year.

Facing page: The archer fish should probably qualify as a tool-using animal. It shoots insects off bankside vegetation by firing a drop of water at them, using a groove in its mouth as a gun barrel and the pressure of its gills as a propellant. It also instinctively knows how to aim off twelve degrees to allow for the angle of refraction where light meets water.

The Enchanted Isles

Though most animals that have colonised the Galapagos Islands belong to a Galapagos species or sub-species, most of its sea birds are found throughout the tropical oceans. Among these are three booby species, the masked, blue-footed and red-footed boobies, all relatives of the more familiar gannet. All three occupy different nesting and feeding niches. Perhaps the most unusual, for a sea-bird anyway, is the red-footed which nests in trees.

I f penguins and fur seals are cold-water species, why are both living and breeding on the equator? This is just one of the many strange phenomena in the Galapagos Islands, off the west coast of South America in the Pacific Ocean.

The islands of the Galapagos lie 600 miles (965 km) west of their parent country Ecuador. The nearest source of both fur seals and penguins lies far to the south on the South American mainland. So what enticed them so far north, and away from the chilly waters they normally frequent? They would never have made the journey, let alone stayed when they reached the islands, had they not encountered the Humboldt or Peru Current, a powerful ocean-flow that pulses up the west coast of South America bringing great volumes of cold water from the Antarctic.

The pattern of deep ocean currents is complex. Apart from the Humboldt Current, the best known is the warm Gulf Stream that governs much of our weather in the North Atlantic. In the eastern Atlantic the Benguela Current affects the west coast of Africa as the Humboldt influences South America, bringing cold water, rich in nutrients, from the Southern Ocean. Of all these complex currents there is only one that is really global. This is the circumpolar current that flows clockwise around the Antarctic. When the Humboldt Current reaches a point roughly parallel with the Galapagos Islands, it meets the South Equatorial Current and is deflected westward towards the archipelago. At this point there are further upwellings of seabed nutrients that greatly enrich the cold waters now flowing towards the Galapagos. Ancient navigators knew about these currents, even if they did not understand their

The Galapagos archipelago is volcanic in origin, as one of the older and more northerly islands, Tower, or Genovesa, clearly shows. Small boats enter Darwin Bay, an old crater, by the seaward gap in the wall. Other smaller craters lie on the plateau-like top of the island.

workings. The first person to sight the Galapagos was the Bishop of Panama, blown and swept off course on a voyage from Panama to Peru in 1535. In fact the winds and currents that surrounded the Galapagos were so tricky and confusing that the Spanish navigators who followed the bishop christened the islands *Las Encantadas* (the Enchanted Isles) because they were so difficult to find.

Like the Hawaiian Chain or the Aleutians, the Galapagos are born of volcanoes. They lie close to the junction of the Pacific, Nazca, and Cocos Plates. Geologists and vulcanists talk of volcanic 'hot spots' where the molten rock breaks through the point at which the earth's moving plates meet. The islands of Isabela and Fernandina, at the westerly end of the archipelago, lie directly over one of these hot spots. Not surprisingly, both islands are highly volcanic. Fernandina consists of one gigantic volcano and its lava beds. A few miles away, is Isabela, the largest island in the group, which has no fewer than five active volcanoes.

The islands to the east of this hot spot were at one time highly volcanic, but the Nazca Plate, on which the Galapagos sit, is moving at the rate of 3 in (7.6 cm) a year away from the main source of vulcanism towards the coast of Ecuador. The easterly islands are therefore old and cold. At the present rate they will have disappeared under the mainland of South America, or at least beneath the waves, in about 20 million years. But by then, of course, it is highly likely that the volcanic hot spot will have given birth to new islands. The volcanic process that created the Galapagos has been continuing for about 10 million years. The undersea lava platforms built up sufficiently for the first islands to break through the surface about 5 million years ago. Some islands are still quite young, being born merely 1–2 million years ago. In total, the undersea volcanoes and fissures oozing molten rock have created 13 main islands and over 40 rocks, small craters and islets that form the archipelago.

Everything about the Galapagos is fascinating both to scientist and layman. Almost every animal is unique to the islands, with the exception of some seabirds which, naturally, range far and wide across the oceans. If an animal or plant is not accorded the status of being a separate species, then it is almost certainly a Galapagos sub-species. The penguins and the fur seals have both been in the islands long enough to become new species, having modified themselves considerably to adapt to local conditions. Galapagos sealions are an example of a sub-species. They are slightly smaller than their ancestors which almost certainly reached the islands from California, lured by the current that flows south from those waters.

It is easy to see how large aquatic creatures, such as sealions and fur seals, made the first voyage to the Enchanted Isles, but not so easy to visualise how some of the terrestrial animals arrived. These were the animals that fired Charles Darwin's imagination when he

The more westerly islands like Isabela and Fernandina lie over the still extremely active volcanic hot spot. Eruptions are frequent and many of the lava floes look as though they cooled only yesterday. In some cases this is true. The climate of the islands causes little erosion of the fantastic rope-like patterns in the lava.

spent a mere five weeks here, visiting with the survey ship *HMS Beagle*, in 1835. Darwin, then a young naturalist, was mainly concerned with iguanas, finches and giant tortoises. His observations contributed greatly to much of the thinking that years later upset the scientific and religious world with his publication *On the Origin of Species*.

During Darwin's five-week visit he noted how the finches had altered to make use of every available source of food. The 13 species, undoubtedly descended from one ancestral mainland finch, had evolved differently shaped beaks to make the best possible use of the seeds and insects available. The most amazing finch of all (which Darwin did not see) is the woodpecker finch, some of which have learned to use a twig or a cactus spine to winkle grubs and insects out of rotten trees.

Not only had 13 different species derived from a common ancestor, but each of these species had evolved slightly differently on different islands to meet local needs. The same was true of the mocking birds which produced four separate island races. Clearly both finches and mocking birds had originally reached the islands by flying, perhaps aided by strong winds, a very considerable distance over the sea. Once there, local winds and currents kept them isolated on their respective islands. So each adapted in minor

Where a woodpecker would use its long sticky tongue to winkle grubs out of trees, the woodpecker finch found it could get the same result by probing with a twig or broken-off cactus spine. Not all woodpecker finches have mastered the trick.

ways to the conditions on their new island. This process became known as natural selection, or survival of the fittest. Incidentally, the ancestor of the finches is thought by modern scientists to have been an insignificant little bird of Central and South America called the blue-black grassquit. It is still common there.

The reptiles on the islands could only have arrived by sea. Darwin was fascinated by the two Galapagos iguanas. The larger is the yellowish land iguana, a vegetarian that feeds amongst other things on prickly pear, or *Opuntia*, a Galapagos sub-species. Its close relative is the most fascinating lizard in the world. The marine iguana grazes on algae on the seabed. It is an accomplished swimmer, its tail having flattened over the years to propel it when swimming either on the surface or submerged. This blackish, rather nightmarish-looking lizard sometimes feeds on the bottom as much as 850 yds (777 m) offshore. It can even drink sea water, though it needs to expel the salt which it does by ejecting a fine spray from the nostrils. There is little doubt that the common ancestor of these two, now widely different, species was the green iguana of the South American mainland.

Although green iguanas are excellent swimmers, it is highly improbable that the original colonists swam all the way from the mainland. It is far more likely that they rafted to the Galapagos on the dense islands of floating vegetation which the mainland rivers discharge into the sea when they flood. Most of these rafts sink when a few miles out into the Pacific. Scientists have calculated, however, that it would only be necessary for one raft carrying a

Darwin noted that the Galapagos mocking birds had evolved in four slightly different ways to meet living and feeding conditions on different islands. What they all have in common is that they are intensely curious and greedy, as scientists camping on the islands find out. Nothing deters them from pilfering and cleaning up cooking utensils.

male and female iguana, or more probably one gravid female, to make a successful landfall once every 100,000 years to have produced the present population. At its peak, the marine iguana population of the islands is approximately 85,000.

The story of immigration by sea and subsequent sub-species diversification is repeated with the Galapagos giant tortoises. Tortoises can stay alive for a long time when floating, even when immersed in salt water. However, the rafting theory is equally valid in their case. Their mainland ancestor is thought to be the small South American tortoise, the *Geochelone*. The original settlers may even have arrived, or sailed part of the way, on a tree trunk or raft of vegetation. Their evolution, since colonising the islands, is almost as spectacular as that of the iguanas. In the first place they became giants. An adult Galapagos tortoise can weigh as much as 350 lb (158 kg), although there is nothing particularly unusual about this. Reptiles on mid-oceanic islands sometimes take on gigantic forms because they face very little competition for food supplies. The tortoises of Aldabra in the Indian Ocean have taken the same evolutionary path. The interesting point about the Galapagos giants is that the carapace, or shell, of each island race is a different shape. This fact was pointed out to Darwin by the governor of the Galapagos, who deserves credit for his powers of observation. To Darwin it was yet one more indication of how natural selection worked. For example, the tortoises of Santa Cruz have flattish, domed shells because the vegetation on which they feed in the comparatively lush highlands of that island is at ground level and easily reached. The Hood Island, or Espanola, tortoises (most Galapagos islands have both British and Ecuadorian names)

The Galapagos marine iguana is the only sea-going lizard in the world. The marine iguana feeds on algae on the seabed. Its tail has become flattened vertically to aid swimming. Its blackish colouration, except when it becomes reddish in the breeding season, perfectly matches the shoreline lava. The dark colour also helps it to absorb heat when emerging from the water.

have a carapace that is high and arched at the front because they feed largely on prickly pear. To reach the food they have to reach upwards with their long necks. This would be hard, if not impossible, with a shell that was low at the front.

Though many of the seabirds that feed around, and nest on, the Galapagos can be found throughout much of the Pacific – for instance the blue-footed and red-footed boobies, frigate birds, and petrels – there are endemic species, too.

The Galapagos penguin must surely take pride of place, if only because it is the only penguin to live as far north as the equator. There are only a few thousand of these little birds in the world, and they nest mainly around the Bolivar Channel between the islands of Isabela and Fernandina. Their choice is based on temperature. Galapagos penguins only breed when the water temperature is around 24°C (75°F). They closely resemble their ancestors on the mainland, though they have taken the opposite route in terms of size to the tortoises. In becoming a separate Galapagos species they have also become a good deal smaller than the original stock from which they sprang. Once again, it is an ocean current that

The giant tortoises of the Galapagos have evolved from a common mainland ancestor to meet living conditions on various islands. Perched on top of this tortoise is a vermilion flycatcher.

This giant Santa Cruz tortoise grazing in the moist uplands of the island weighs around 350 lb. Giant forms are thought to develop on isolated oceanic islands because of the lack of competition.

Facing page: This bright blue foot performs other important functions besides walking, swimming and, as here, preening. In courtship the male bluefooted booby makes much of showing off his blue footwear to the female, principally in his display flight when coming in to land. He 'flashes' his webbed feet at her before touching down.

restricts them to this one part of the islands. The east-flowing Cromwell, or Equatorial undercurrent, that races between the islands of Fernandina and Isabela, is not only rich in nutrients from upwellings from the seabed, it is also agreeably cold.

In the same area nests one of the oceans' strangest birds, the Galapagos flightless cormorant. This large cormorant species discovered long ago that it did not need to waste energy by flying. All the food it needed was obtainable by diving, and there were no predators to worry about. Unlike the penguin, the cormorant does not use its residual wings to move underwater. When submerged it propels itself by means of powerful webbed feet. Although there are perhaps only 400 of this species in the world (all nest around the Bolivar Channel) they appear to be in no danger, though conceivably a catastrophe in this highly volcanic area of the islands could endanger them. Should this ever happen, man would probably have to intervene. Volcanic cataclysm was not something natural selection took into account when it decided that the cormorant no longer needed to fly!

The little Galapagos penguin is the most northerly of its kind. Although penguins are normally cold water birds, the presence of cold water currents in the Galapagos allows this species to nest on the equator.

There are two other examples of seabirds that reached the islands long ago, and stayed to evolve into unique Galapagos species. One is the beautiful swallowtail gull. With forked tail and long pointed wings, it is more like a tern than a gull. It is so unlike all other gulls that it is given a separate genus of its own. The swallowtail is also the only gull that feeds exclusively at night, probably to escape aerial enemies, particularly the robbing and raiding frigate birds.

The other unique Galapagos gull is the lava gull, a rather drab-looking bird that matches the blue-grey of the lava from which it takes its name. Its closest mainland relative is the laughing gull. Like most gulls it lives by scavenging. There are only 400 pairs of lava gulls in the entire world, and they are all found here.

The Galapagos are without doubt a significant part of our world heritage and they need the world's protection. Ecuador, to whom the islands belong, is justly proud of them and shows every sign of keeping their ocean eco-systems intact. Unfortunately mankind's record in these precious islands was, until a few years ago, exceedingly black. In the late seventeenth century, the pirates and buccaneers raiding the Spanish cities of the mainland used them as a refuge. The islands were too far away for Spanish ships intent on revenge.

The pirates used to run their ships ashore for a refit, landing them on the beaches. In one of the few coves that provided a safe anchorage, the graffiti of early visitors – largely in the form of ships' names and dates – can still be seen, scratched on the lava cliffs. The legacy left by the pirates was a horde of rats that escaped from their ships' holds to breed ashore. They have never been eradicated and probably never will be. The rats, brown and black, inflict enormous damage on the Galapagos wildlife that has never perfected defences against mammalian predators.

From 1780 to 1860, British and American sealers and whalers invaded the islands. The whalers remorselessly hunted the sperm whales until the Galapagos whaling grounds were described by one captain as 'dry cruising'. But the most significant damage inflicted by both sealers and whalers was to fill their holds with giant tortoises, usually the females that were smaller and could be crammed into a tighter space. Tortoise meat was excellent, particularly when it was fresh, which involved occasional feedings for up to a year to keep them alive. It is estimated that in 80 years the hunters caught over 1,000 tortoises. They took them not only for food but for their fat, which provided cooking oil. While the sealers also caught tortoises, they made colossal inroads on the fur seal population. One captain, Benjamin Morrel, recorded that he

Penguins and Galapagos flightless cormorants share the same nesting area around the islands of Fernandina and Isabela where they get the benefits of the cold, eastward-flowing Cromwell current. They sometimes nest on the same lava rocks, not always peaceably.

77

killed 5,000 fur seals in two months. By the early 1930s, the Galapagos fur seal had been almost exterminated for its fur and underlying skin. Only at the very last moment was it protected. Fortunately the fur seal population has now totally recovered. It is, however, noticeable that Galapagos fur seals are rather more wary of man than are the Galapagos sealions which, like every other creature living there, are completely tame.

Some of the damage, notably that inflicted by the feral descendants of dogs, cats and goats (mainly introduced by settlers), can probably never be completely undone. But Ecuador, with international help, has made great strides in conservation. In 1959 it declared the islands a national park. And in 1964 Ecuador gained a powerful international ally, with the Charles Darwin Foundation opening a research station on the island of Santa Cruz. Scientists from all over the world now come to study the conservation problems of the islands. National Park guides are trained at the Darwin Station to take small parties of tourists on carefully defined trails over some of the islands.

Endangered island sub-species of iguanas and tortoises are bred in captivity at the Darwin Station for reintroduction to the islands, where their numbers have fallen critically. Reintroduction is not carried out, however, until every attempt has been made to eliminate or at least reduce the numbers of predators that caused the decline. This is a tremendous task, because on the rough lava terrain of many of the islands it is practically impossible to eliminate feral cats and goats.

The overall aim is to keep the Galapagos as close to its natural original state as possible. It will not be easy. There are at present approximately 10,000 Ecuadorian settlers living on just four of the

Probably the most elegant gull in the world, the swallowtail gull of the Galapagos is also the only one to feed nocturnally. It may have developed this habit in order to escape the piratical attentions of the frigate birds.

larger islands. In addition, over 25,000 tourists, many Ecuadorian, visit the Galapagos each year, with the numbers still rising. Domestic pets are also likely to escape and become feral predators. There is always the risk, too, that non-indigenous insects or plants will be introduced in cargoes or even on visitors' clothing, to the detriment of the Galapagos habitat. It is extremely difficult to keep an entire archipelago in what amounts to ecological mothballs, but the attempt is being made with considerable energy and creditable determination.

There are some forces of destruction which are beyond mankind's power to stop or even alleviate. *El Niño* is one of them. *El Niño* is a warm-water ocean current that flows down the coast of Central America from the north, and then turns westward joining the

Nobody knows for sure who Sally Lightfoot was, but this crab which can be seen scuttling over the rocks, and sometimes appearing to skate over the water, is named after her. One story is that the original was a Spanish dancer.

79

In a sub-marine cave Galapagod fur seals perform a water ballet silhouetted against the surface light.

South Equatorial Current. It arrives each year, just before Christmas, and is named after the Christ child.

Every few years, *El Niño* flows in such volume that it pushes the rich cold waters of the Humboldt Current away from the coast. They take with them the organisms on which fish feed, so robbing the local fishing industry and the seabirds of precious food supplies. Its effects, even in 'tame' years, are felt in the Galapagos. The blazing equatorial sun is often hidden by an overcast sky. The water round the most southerly of the islands warms up and seals, sealions and seabirds find it harder to get a good living.

The year when *El Niño* went really wild was 1982. The volume of warm water grew and grew, and not only pushed out westwards into the Pacific, but pushed halfway across the ocean. In the Galapagos the effect was immediate. For months on end the islands were covered by cloud. Very little rain falls each year in the lowland areas, but in 1982 rainfall was continual and tropical. The plankton swarms and the fish that feed on them moved away, and warm water replaced cold. Seabirds failed to nest. Vegetation grew on islands that were normally bare. The corpses of marine iguanas littered the shorelines. Sealions and fur seals failed to breed. Any pups that were born died because their mothers could not catch the fish that would have produced the milk the pups needed.

Drastic as were *El Niño*'s effects upon the Galapagos, they were but a pinprick compared to what that flood of warm water across the Pacific did to the entire weather system of the southern hemisphere. *El Niño* was responsible for floods in Ecuador, and droughts in southern Africa and even Australia. That destructive *El Niño* year illustrates better than any other event that ocean and land are parts of the same great organism.

The year 1982 showed how rapidly nature can repair itself, if given the chance. By 1984 *El Niño* was behaving itself once more. The plankton shoals and the fish that feed on them had returned to the Galapagos. Seabird, sealion, fur seal, and marine iguana populations were back to strength. But even with *El Niño*'s benign influence this probably could not have happened had not the breeding beaches and lava cliffs of the Galapagos received complete protection. Onslaught by man and nature is usually too much for any eco-system to withstand.

There is more than one marine iguana in this picture. The camouflage is perfect against the background of driftwood and lava.

The People of the Sea

P erhaps because marine mammals are warm-blooded like ourselves, they seem to have a special place in our regard. Whales are the current object of our reverence and affection. We have accredited the unprepossessing dugong and manatee (the so-called sea cows) with providing us with the legend of the mermaid. We are delighted by the cuddly and clever Pacific sea otter, which belongs to that select company of tool-using animals (by virtue of being able to crack open its hard-shelled sea food with a stone). As for the last group of marine mammals, the seals, they have always had a dual relationship with man, mixing fondness and death.

In the recent past man has hunted many species of seals with complete ruthlessness. The sad fact is that the reverse side of our admiration for marine mammals is the desire to exploit them, even to extinction. This is also true of the whales and their lesser relatives, the dolphins. Meanwhile, the dugong and manatee are hanging on in small numbers by the flat of their tails.

The fur trade thought it had extinguished the sea otter, until a relict population was discovered off the California coast in 1938. Later, sea otters were found to be alive and thriving in fair numbers off Alaska. But in 1989 a large section of the Alaskan population was killed when the tanker *Exxon Valdes* with its cargo of crude oil, hit a reef in Prince Rupert Sound. They survived the pollution. The love–hate relationship with seals persists, though fortunately now with more love than hate. However, our attitude to the creatures sometimes called the People of the Sea is, to put it mildly, still ambivalent, especially when they compete with our own interests.

The walrus may look like one of Nature's jokes but every-thing has a purpose. The ivory tusks are for rooting about on the seabed after molluscs and the bristly hairs assess whether what the tusks have uncovered is edible.

82

Viewed from this angle, the manatee is an unlikely candidate for being the inspiration of the mermaid legend. The flattened tail is said to have been responsible. Manatees can grow to eleven feet. They feed on water plants.

The appeal seals have for people lies mainly in their faces and more particularly their eyes. The latter are often described as being doglike. They have the moist appealing look of a labrador, and there is something gratifyingly human about the shape of the head. There is considerable evidence that the animals we find most appealing are the ones that most resemble ourselves, and have an almost human look. Scientists may find this regrettably anthropomorphic, but it is nonetheless true. The Disney organisation did considerable research into the shapes of cartoon characters with which the audience most empathised. Round, baby-like features and eyes scored heavily. Mickey Mouse is the embodiment of this round 'friendliness'. So, to a very large extent, are seals.

In the Outer Hebrides where the Scottish islanders have hunted seals for their skins, flesh and oil for at least 8,000 years, they superstitiously believed that there was only one seal, and that you killed it over and over again. If you did not have a proper respect for your quarry it would not be there next time you needed it.

Yet superstition went further and far deeper than that. When a seal hunter was drowned, which must have been a frequent occurrence in those stormy northern seas, the locals believed that a seal came ashore to console his widow and perhaps father the child he could not longer provide. This convenient story has been preserved in many north country ballads. The words vary but the theme is always the same. Here is one version:

> I heard a mother dancing her bairn,
> And aye she'd rock it and she'd sing
> 'Oh, little ken I my bairnie's dad
> Nor yet the land that he lives in.
> Then in there came a great grey seal
> And laid himself down at her feet
> 'I'll tell you where his daddy is –
> He's lying down here at your feet.
> I am a man upon the land,
> I am a seal when I'm in the sea;
> And when I'm far from every strand
> My home is in the north country'.

Today the California population of sea otters is flourishing. Local fishermen complain that the otters eat abalone, a valuable commercial shellfish. Otters also eat sea urchins which eat the kelp beds in which both abalone and otters live.

Note that the ballad referred to the grey seal, one of the two species found in British waters. The other is the common, or harbour, seal. The male grey seal, with its Roman nose, has a particularly human-like profile which perhaps contributed to the legend.

Seals belong to the order *Pinnipedia*. The order contains a mere 17 genera, an extremely small number when compared with, say, the order *Carnivora* (93 genera) or the order *Rodentia* (393 genera). Worldwide there are only 32 species of seals.

The *Pinnipedia* are divided into two superfamilies. You can immediately distinguish them by the way they 'walk'. Anyone who has seen a sealion performing in a circus or lumbering over the rocks in a zoo enclosure will know that its back flippers are divided so that they can be turned foward, giving the animal almost a four-footed movement when ashore. Sealions belong to the superfamily *Otarioidea*, as do the fur seals and walruses. They can all turn their flippers forward to act as rather crude hind legs. Just to make things slightly more confusing, the superfamily is divided into two families, the sealions and fur seals (*Otariidae*) and the walruses (*Odobenidae*). There are other not so obvious anatomical features exclusive to members of this superfamily. The most apparent is that they all have small external ears. Also, they are all exclusively marine species.

In 1989, the tanker Exxon Valdez, *heading for the Alaskan oil terminal at the head of Prince Rupert Sound, hit a reef and spilled millions of gallons of crude oil. Sea otters, fish and birds were wiped out and the marine environment was damaged for years to come.*

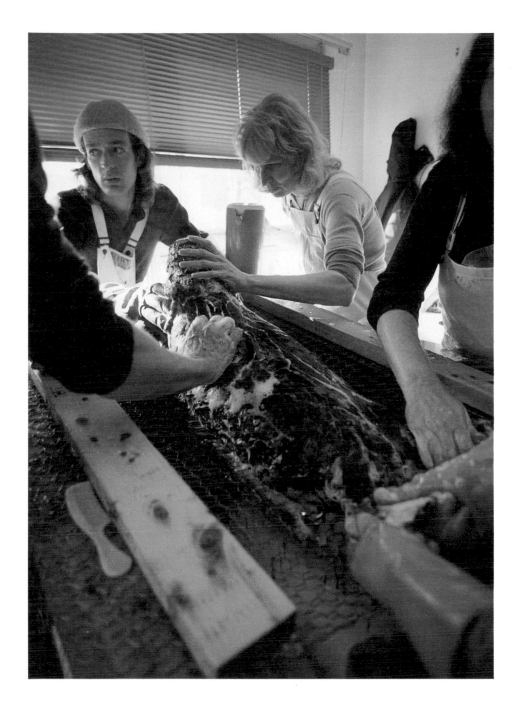

It is possible to remove the crude oil from a sea otter's rich coat but not from its guts once it has ingested it. A few were saved after the Exxon Valdez *disaster but not many.*

The other superfamily is the *Phocoidea* or, as they are often called, the 'true seals'. They are unable to manipulate their rear flippers in order to 'walk'. Whereas the size of the nails in the other superfamily differ in size, in the *Phocoidea* the nails are the same size on each digit. Members of the true seal superfamily may be found in marine, estuarine or even freshwater habitats. The Lake Baikal seal lives exclusively in fresh water.

The land-living ancestors of the seals returned to the ocean when the whales had already established themselves there for millions of years. It is believed that they have only been marine mammals for half as long as the whales and dolphins. The ancestor of the seal and sealion was, in all likelihood, a bear-like creature. Evidence of its shorter tenure of the seas is that all seals have to come ashore to give birth, whereas the whales mate and bear their calves in the ocean. Seals have therefore not become entirely independent of the land.

Nevertheless, seals have solved most of the problems facing warm-blooded animals that have chosen to live in cold, often freezing water. While a whale relies largely on size and thick coatings of blubber to keep warm, many seals only weigh around 200 lb (97 kg) and therefore cannot carry the same thickness of insulation. Instead, seals have a cunningly insulated circulatory system. The arteries that carry the warm blood to the extremities, such as the flippers, where you would expect heat loss to be the greatest, are surrounded by veins. The cooler blood in the veins

The face that has always struck a chord of sympathy with man, even though in many cases he has done his best to obliterate its owner. Is it the doglike eyes and rounded features that make seals so appealing? Our attitudes towards them are improving – but only just in time.

absorbs some of the warmth from the arterial blood and carries it back so that it does not escape to the surface. This is particularly evident in species such as the Weddell seal that lives on, or under, the Antarctic pack ice. The fur seal which frequents rather warmer, though still chilly waters wears a thick velvety coat that has 300,000 hairs to 1 sq in (6.5 cm²). This is why it was so remorselessly hunted by the fur trade.

Seals have acquired a strange and varied glossary of descriptive terms. Perhaps because they are so widely distributed about the world they have become a large part of seafaring not to say hunting folklore. A large congregation of seals is often referred to as a herd, though when it is a breeding colony it becomes a rookery (a term also applied to penguin colonies). Adult males are bulls, the females cows, which the master bull collects in harems. An infant seal is a pup, but on reaching one year old becomes, like a horse, a

In America it is called a harbour seal. In Britain it is known as the Common Seal. In the Pacific they occur everywhere from the north shore of Alaska to Mexico, in the Atlantic from Greenland to South Carolina, and they are also plentiful in the North Sea.

yearling. Immature and non-breeding males are fairly logically called bachelors. Nursery groups of pups are often referred to as pods. Terms with which I was unfamiliar until I read Judith E. King's *Seals of the World* (British Museum of Natural History, 1964) are wig and clapmatch. Apparently these are sealers' words for breeding males and females respectively. Best of all, and from the same source, is bedlamer, meaning a young harp or hooded seal. Apparently this is a corruption of the name given to these seals by the Breton settlers in Canada in the sixteenth century. They called them *bête de la mer*.

Seals come in a variety of sizes. The largest of the sealions, Steller's sealion from the North Pacific, is one of the giants. An adult male can measure 10½ ft (3.2 m) nose to tail, and weigh 1 tonne. The largest of the *Pinnipedia*, the male elephant seal which ranges from northern California to South Georgia in the sub-

Unlike common seals whose pups are born between the tides and have to swim straight away, grey seals have a much longer rearing period. The pups who are born with a white coat remain helpless for around six weeks.

Facing page: Every single one of these walruses 'hauled out' on Round Island, off the coast of Alaska, is a male. Although walruses mate in summer, they spend most of the season in separate groups. They even migrate separately, males in one group, females and calves in another.

Antarctic, sometimes reaches an overall length of 20 ft (6 m) and weighs up to 8,000 lb (3.6 tonne). The far smaller cows tip the scales at a mere 2,000 lb (907 kg). Walruses, which are found in fairly shallow seas around the Arctic coasts of the Atlantic and Pacific, are comparative lightweights, an adult male reaching 3,000 lb (1.4 tonne) and the slightly smaller female 1,800 lb (816 kg). Contrast this with the common seal of British waters (in Canada and Alaska it is known as the harbour seal) whose maximum weight is around 250 lb (113 kg).

Seals, generally speaking, are fish-eaters, which is one of the main reasons why they find themselves at odds with man, especially when they become partial to a species commercially valuable such as the Atlantic and Pacific salmon. Generally, the seals' seafood menu is very varied, featuring squid, flounders, crabs, mussels, lamprey, cod and even, in the case of the predatory leopard seal of Antarctic and sub-Atlantic seas, penguins. I have seen sealion bulls chase and catch penguins in the Falkland Islands,

shaking them as a terrier shakes a rat until flesh is torn loose from the skin. This is rather how a leopard seal kills though it does so with greater dexterity.

People often ask why a walrus has tusks. What does it use them for? A popular though incorrect theory is that it employs them to give itself a grip on the ice when hauling itself out of the water. In fact the tusks are upper canine teeth. The male's, which are larger than the female's, have been known to reach nearly 40 in (1 m) in length and weigh up to 12 lb (5.5 kg). They are made of ivory, whose granular nature is clearly distinguished from elephant ivory when used in carvings. To the walrus, these enlarged canine teeth are a means of stirring up bottom mud when searching for the molluscs on which it feeds. Yet fragments of shell are not found in the stomachs of walruses because once the tusks have uncovered the shellfish, lips and whiskers home in on the food. Feet and fleshy siphons are torn off and swallowed, and the shell is discarded. A walrus can even take a mussel into its mouth, suck out the soft, edible parts and reject the shell.

Seals have three main predators. In temperate seas they, and particularly their pups, often fall prey to sharks. Killer whales range most waters, even as far as the Arctic and Antarctic pack ice. At Peninsular Valdes, in Patagonia, 400 miles (643 km) south of Buenos Aires, killer whales weighing well over 1 tonne regularly snatch young elephant seals from the breeding beaches, making their attacks in just a few inches of water, right amongst the breaking surf. Until very recently man was the greatest predator of all. As recounted in previous chapters, the sealers came very close to wiping out many of the fur seal and elephant seal rookeries of the sub-Antarctic, as well as the Galapagos Islands, not to mention the prolific breeding colonies of the northern fur seal in the Pribilof Islands in the Bering Sea, between Russia and Alaska.

When the islands were first discovered by the Russian navigator Gerassim Pribilof in 1786, the local fur seal population numbered approximately 2½ million. By 1911, excessive sealing had reduced numbers to approximately 200,000 animals, under one tenth of the original population. If sealing had not been checked and regulated by agreement between the USA, Russia, Great Britain and Japan, numbers could easily have fallen further to danger level.

The agreement was broken in 1941 by the wartime withdrawal of Japan. In 1952 Canada, Japan and the USA launched a joint programme of research into the status of the Pribilof fur seals, and five years later the four original signatories signed a new convention. Consequently, the fur seals soon reached their maximum numbers. This figure even allowed for a regulated cropping programme by the United States Wildlife Service, in which 60,000–70,000 animals were culled annually. The cull was confined to bachelors since this did not disrupt the breeding structure of the herd. The young males also have the best skins, of which Canada and Japan received 15 per cent. The carcasses were used for chicken

meal and the blubber was refined for soap manufacture. Though such a process may seem shocking, it is a perfect example of well-managed conservation. The species concerned is kept at optimum levels and there are fringe benefits and spin-offs, including some hunting rights for native peoples. In 1972 it was found that the fur seal numbers were falling alarmingly for an unknown reason and the culling was stopped.

The same could not be said for the annual slaughter of baby harp seals in the Gulf of St Lawrence, off the Atlantic coast of Canada. The white-coated pups are born on the ice. At birth they are of little value to the fur trade, but between 2–10 days old this white coat is at its best. After that, the white hairs start to fall out. Since the baby pelt is naturally less valuable if marked or damaged, the traditional way of killing the pups for their skins is by hitting them over the head with a wooden club, resembling a baseball bat. Some years as many as 180,000 pups were killed in this way, with the sealing vessels arriving from as far away as Scandinavia. The battle to stop this annual slaughter of the innocents, as the press called it, lasted for 20 years. It was fought by many people, but no individual or organisation argued more strongly or doggedly than the International Fund for Animal Welfare and its Welsh founder, Brian Davies. Finally, the import of baby harp seal skins was

A female grey seal has no breeding territory. She moves around and the pup moves with her. A cow suckles her pup for around 18 days.

93

banned internationally and the extensive slaughter ceased. Unfortunately, the Norwegians continue to kill on the ice east of Greenland and show no signs of stopping.

Within the bounds of this chapter it is impossible to describe the breeding biology of each of the oceans' 32 seal species. Fortunately, the two species familiar in Britain are conveniently and interestingly different. Both also occur across the Atlantic and one in the Pacific. The common or harbour seal is found in Britain mainly on the east coast, though there are breeding colonies in the Shetlands, Hebrides, and the Bristol Channel. The seal ranges as far north as Iceland and along the coast of Norway to its northernmost point. It is found as far south as the northern shores of Spain.

In the western Atlantic, common seals range from Greenland to South Carolina. In the Pacific, common or harbour seals occur everywhere on the western seaboard from Japan to the north of the Soviet Union, and on the eastern side from the Beaufort Sea (on the northern shore of Alaska) to the far south of California and even into Mexican waters. Though it is hard, if not impossible, to spot external differences, at least five sub-species exist across this vast range.

Common seals are altogether a tubbier, more confiding-looking animal than the grey seal. Unlike the Roman-nosed grey seal, the common seal has a rounded head. If all else fails, you can distinguish it by the V-shaped nostrils, because the grey seal's are vertical and parallel. Its breeding habits are quite different, too. The common seal is an animal that likes sheltered waters. The grey seal is not put off by rocky storm-washed beaches, and even seems to prefer them.

Common seals are, in one way at least, more fully adapted to life in the ocean. Their pups are, literally, born between the tides and can swim at birth. They have to if they are not to drown in the next tide that flows over the sand bank on which most, though not all, are born. Initially the pups have a mottled sea-going coat. The white baby coat in which many seal babies spend the first 10 days or so of their lives has already been shed in the womb. There seems to be a much closer relationship between mother and pup than with grey seals, which lasts about six weeks, double the length of the maternal bond in greys. The ability of mother and pup to be sea-going from birth saved the common seal from over-exploitation in the days of heavy commercial hunting.

Mothers appear to enjoy playing with their young, and often find landing places for them, helping them out of the water onto the seaweed-covered rocks that occur on some of the sheltered sea lochs round which they breed in Scotland. Like all seal pups, they are fed on some of the richest milk in the world. Seal's milk contains up to 50 per cent fat, as against cow's milk which scores only 5 per cent. With this diet they put on weight at the rate of 2 lb (0.9 kg) per day. The pups weigh 20 lb (9 kg) at birth and nearly double this in the first fortnight. They are weaned after four weeks.

The grey seal is a very different animal from the common seal. It occurs on both sides of the Atlantic, but two thirds of the world population of 160,000 lives around British coasts, half the entire population breeding in the Hebrides.

At about the time the common seals leave the shoreline for open water, after breeding and rearing their pups, the grey seals come ashore to begin their breeding season. Some of the most favoured sites are on the Monach Island 5 miles (8 km) west of Benbecula in the Hebrides. The Monachs were sparsely inhabited until 1949

A white-coated grey seal pup.

Virus Scare

In 1988 a mysterious and lethal virus attacked the common seal in the North Sea. Scientists eventually pinned down the cause, a virus called *Morbillivirus*, related to canine distemper. Though it remained unproven, it was suspected that pollution in the North Sea, which has become the dumping ground for the filth of Europe's rivers, may have contributed to the disaster.

Although the grey seals also caught the disease, very few died. In 1988 17,000 grey common seals died, including 67 per cent of Holland's population. Yet in 1989 only 2,000 died. Seal populations recover from such blows remarkably quickly, provided their food supply is available and adverse factors, such as chemical pollution, are not involved. One positive outcome of the common seal virus was the provision of a new weapon with which conservation organisations could attack the many polluters of the North Sea.

when the few shepherds and fishermen moved back to the mainland. Immediately the grey seals moved in. Today the islands have the largest grey seal breeding population in the world, producing up to 4,000 pups a year.

The Monachs are an unusual grey seal breeding habitat, with wide sandy beaches backed by high dunes. Elsewhere, grey seals are often confined by human disturbance to exposed rocky shores.

In September, the seals converge from hundreds of miles around, having been at sea for nearly a year. At first they bob about in the waves as if inspecting the area. Soon 800 seals have hauled themselves out onto a single beach. The immature bulls start to playfight, but this is merely a rehearsal for the real thing. They will not breed this year. In late September, the pregnant cows leave the assembly beaches for the breeding areas nearby where they will give birth, probably in the dunes. Unlike the common seals, the pups are born with a white coat and remain fairly helpless for at least six weeks. The cows have no set breeding territory. The pups move around and the mothers move with them, so their territory is wherever the pup is. The mother feeds her young for around 18 days. During the breeding season both sexes hardly eat. In fact a cow will fast for at least two and a half weeks, and the bulls for up to six weeks. Sadly about one tenth of the pups do not survive, usually because they have become lost through failing to make a strong enough bond with their mothers during the first two or three crucial days.

October is the time where the bulls come into their own. The fights between mature bulls are savage and earnest, with bites often causing severe injuries. At the same period the cows come into season as soon as their pups are weaned. Directly a cow has been mated she heads back to sea.

By late October, the last of the pups has been weaned. They are entirely on their own now. They move up into the dunes to moult, and will not feed again until they go to sea in two or three weeks' time. While a pup is lying up in the dunes, it converts its fat into muscle and moults into its sea coat. At six or seven weeks old it is ready to enter its realm – the kingdom of the deep.

Now that grey seals are no longer hunted commercially, the population is growing at the rate of about 5 per cent a year. This

A mouth 'designed' for catching and holding the seal's slippery prey. The whiskers are sensitive to obstructions but not always sensitive enough to detect the almost invisible gill-nets in which increasing numbers of seals are caught and drowned.

means that the seals are increasingly likely to find themselves in confrontation with man. Fishermen complain that fish stocks are being depleted and that seals are partly responsible. But then fishermen have always made these claims, which in some part are no doubt true. The fishermen of the Farne Islands, off the Northumbrian coast, have always complained that the grey seals who breed there make serious inroads into salmon stocks.

Salmon farming is a new and thriving industry, mainly in Scottish inlets and sea lochs. The salmon are protected by a double row of nets but when the tide pushes the nets together a determined seal can go through them like a torpedo, and cause about as much damage. There is the added danger that thousands of artificially reared salmon will escape and breed with the wild salmon, adversely affecting their offsprings' ability to survive. Until recently the Ministry of Agriculture authorised grey seal culls on North Rona in the Hebrides, but the conservation lobby has managed to stop these, at least for the time being. Clashes like these will continue as long as there are seals and fishermen. Fortunately, now that commercial sealing has virtually stopped, the 'people of the sea' will probably be around as long as the people who live on land.

Sockeye salmon that run the gauntlet of seals along the coast and return to the headwaters of the river of their birth to spawn. Seals have always taken their share of valuable food fish. Pacific salmon like these still exist in great numbers although the Atlantic salmon has fallen on hard times.

The Bear that Goes to Sea

Incredibly, the world's largest land carnivore spends practically its entire life at sea. About a quarter of a million years ago an ancestor of the brown bear discovered a rich alternative food supply by turning its back on the land, and rival predators. Many millions of years previously, the ancestors of the whales and seals had made a similar discovery. They had, however, taken to the water in its liquid form, which demanded considerable physiological modifications. A new streamlined body shape had to be acquired, limbs had to be converted into flippers, and the breathing apparatus, including the lungs, needed to be adapted to sea life.

The bear that went to sea underwent a far easier conversion that was comfortably accomplished in a mere 250,000 years. Part of the reason was that this offshoot of the brown bear family spent most of its year on the Arctic pack ice, not in the sea itself.

Compared with the marine mammals, the bodily adaptations made were relatively straightforward. A white coat was required, not so much to hide the bear from its enemies, for it was so powerful there were few enemies to worry about, but to conceal it from prey when hunting on snow and ice. Since the bear lived for most of the time in sub-zero temperatures the water-repellent coat that it eventually developed overlay fat up to 3 in (7.6 cm) thick. Ear and tail extremities that encouraged heat loss gradually shrunk to the minimum size. And claws needed to be exceptionally sharp for seizing and holding slippery marine prey.

All bears have an excellent sense of smell, but since this predator would seek prey under several feet of ice or snow, scenting powers had to be especially acute. Locomotion on ice and in freezing water

The polar bear is very well insulated for swimming in the cold waters. Its body is elongated for better stream-lined movement.

also demanded certain modifications. For better swimming, the feet became partially webbed. To assist walking and running on ice, the soles of the feet between the pads were equipped with hair to give the heavy animal a good grip. Although bigger than its distant brown bear relatives, the ice bear was less heavily built with a longer and more sinuous head and neck that helped it swim among broken ice. The end result was an animal magnificently geared to one of the harshest environments on earth. American scientists have recently discovered that the hollow hairs of a polar bear's coat can conduct ultra-violet light from their tips down to the bear's black skin. There, by some mechanism not yet understood, it is converted to heat.

The polar bear was not described as a separate species until 1774. The earliest record of polar bears being taken into captivity occurs in AD 880 when two cubs were transported from Iceland to Norway. In 1965 the polar bear expert C.R. Harrington described

The ancestors of the polar bear were a race of brown bears who found there was a good living to be had out on the pack ice. Among the adaptations that had to be made was the acquisition of a white coat and smaller ears to cut down heat loss.

A polar bear passed this way. To give it grip on the ice, a polar bear has hairs on the soles of its feet.

how polar bear cubs were offered to European rulers for their menageries: 'They rewarded the donors on various occasions with ships carrying cargoes of timber or even bishoprics.'

Serious hunting of polar bears had to wait until the seventeenth century when the whalers sailed their ships as far as the pack ice. In the next 200 years, the numbers of bears decreased sharply. The sealers, in characteristic style, accelerated the decline. As recently as 1942 Norwegian sealers alone accounted for 714 polar bears.

The eskimos have always hunted polar bears for their own needs – meat, oil, and clothing – but after World War Two they hunted for pelts and trophies to sell to the outside world. And in the 1950s and early 1960s American and European hunters frequently used light aircraft on skis to land on the ice close to their victims, which they promptly shot. There was very little exertion or risk involved, merely the ability to hold a rifle fairly steady for a close-range kill. In 1965, C.R. Harrington estimated that the world population of bears was down to approximately 10,000, with 1,300 being shot every year.

Polar bears prefer to hunt in areas of broken ice which give cover for the stalk, and open water where their favourite prey, ringed seals, may be found. The bears are excellent swimmers. When hunting they can stay submerged for up to two minutes.

A male polar bear stands between 8–9½ ft (2.4–2.9 m) high, with an average weight of approximately 900 lb (400 kg). The females are smaller and weigh some 200 lb (900 kg) less. Contrary to its awesome reputation, and despite its tremendous strength and agility, the polar bear is not particularly aggressive to humans. And because of the impenetrability of its habitat on the pack ice, it has, until recently, had little contact with people and has not therefore had time to acquire a built-in fear reaction. Though there are undoubtedly situations in which a polar bear can become extremely dangerous, there is no record of a bear killing a human as prey, let alone eating the flesh. However, all bears are curious and inquisitive, especially where stores of food are concerned. Brown and grizzly bears, who have had far more cause to fear man, are highly unpredictable and are liable to charge without apparent reason. Polar bears do not seem to share these alarming characteristics. There have even been cases of the animals coming right up to a sealer on the ice, sniffing him, and, when the man has shouted for help, turning tail and plunging into the water.

The kingdom of the polar bear is the Arctic Ocean, an area approximately the size of Europe. There are five nations that play host to polar bears – the USA (Alaska), Canada (the north and east coasts, as far south as Hudson Bay), Denmark (Greenland), Sweden (Svalbard, formerly Spitzbergen) and the USSR. There have even been rare sightings of bears in Japan.

Polar bears are solitary animals, except for females escorting cubs, although as many as 30 have been seen together scavenging a whale carcass. Interestingly, this occurs without the squabbling and snarling characteristic of other large predators on a kill. The bears' movements are largely governed by the ice drift on the ocean currents, east to west round the pole. During the Arctic winter the bears live and hunt on the ice in total darkness, relying on their sense of smell and what little light is reflected from the ice and snow to help them locate their prey. Seals form the polar bear's staple diet.

The bears prefer to hunt in the area of broken ice where the wind and currents keep the pack in motion. Hunting bears tend to congregate where there is a mixture of heavy, piled-up ice, newly frozen ice, and stretches of open water known as 'leads'. These are where the seals can be found. The blocks of ice piled up by the pressure of grinding floes provide ideal cover from which to stalk any seal that has emerged from the water.

Polar bears are not only excellent swimmers, but can stay underwater for up to two minutes when hunting. The usual technique when making a swimming attack is to slide into the water, hind legs first, dive just before coming in range of the victim, and then spring out of the water onto the floe to cut off the seal's line of escape. Bears also wait patiently by the breathing holes in the ice which the seals keep open by constant use. They

The entrance to a polar bear's den, usually dug on a slope. Cubs are born in December and January and are kept warm by the mother's fur and the insulation of the den.

The indiscriminate shooting of polar bears has now largely been stopped but quite a number of bears are still killed each year on the pretext that they are a nuisance. Eskimo settlements are allowed to kill a certain number of bears annually. These drying skins will be used by eskimos for clothing.

The den has a passage 6½–19½ ft (2–6 m) long. At the end of this is an open space approximately 8 ft (2½ m) long, 5 ft (1½ m) wide, and 5 ft (1½ m) high. The occupant's body heat keeps the 'room' temperature around freezing point, when outside it may be anything down to 40 degrees below zero.

On Wrangel Island in the Soviet Arctic, Russian scientists have located 150 caves which the bears use for winter denning, the occupants returning to the same caves each year. The further north the habitat, the colder the weather, and the less chance there is of finding any food. The further north they travel, therefore, the more males go into a state of winter rest. However, all pregnant females, no matter how far north or south their range, build themselves a den and tuck themselves into it to overwinter.

The cubs (usually two, the numbers varying from one to, rarely, three) are born in December and January. At birth they are about 1 ft (0.3 m) long and weigh approximately 1½ lb (0.7 kg). Most of the known facts about the polar bear's breeding biology were, until very recently, learned from captive bears in zoos. Now, more and more scientific studies of the five polar bear nations are being carried out in the field.

The cubs have a coating of short hair when born, open their eyes at 33 days, but do not develop perfect hearing until 69 days. They are ready to walk by the 47th day. The mother, throughout this period, when she is feeding her young, receives no food herself and lives off the accumulated store of fat from her rich summer diet.

When the weather starts to turn milder in March, the females and cubs leave the den but remain close to it for some days. In fine weather the young play, sliding down snow banks, and dig for plants, imitating their mother. At any sign of danger or at the onset of severe weather, the family returns to the den.

Since the mother soon feels the need to feed she heads for the sealing grounds with the cubs. They keep up with her, sometimes for long distances at a stretch, usually following in line astern but, in areas of deep snow, running by her side. Apparently this prevents them from stumbling and falling into her deep footprints.

At first the mother concentrates on catching young seals. When she is approaching prey, the young stay safely in the rear, until it is clear the victim is not dangerous. Later, she shares the dead seals with her cubs, although she is still suckling them, often resting on a safe ice block to do so. She is careful not to take her family into the icy sea until winter is well past, and then only when strictly necessary.

As the cubs grow in confidence and ability, she leads them further and further away from the coast and out onto the ice. It is quite rare for a female to spend the first summer with her family on land, because land is far more dangerous than ice. Wolves are one problem. Although a female can put up stiff resistance in defending her family, she usually chooses to flee with the cubs. If the pursuit

This well-grown cub will spend a second winter in the den with its mother. During that time it will grow its adult teeth but will be suckled by its mother until it is 21 months old.

Flight of the Snowgeese, had one nerve-wracking experience with a large male bear. The Bartletts had reared a family of orphaned snowgeese for the film. At night they brought the goslings inside their tent to protect them from predators. One full moon Des was asleep, naked, inside his Arctic goose-down sleeping bag when he heard a scratching and snuffling outside the tent. He sat up and saw a long shadow cast across the tent roof. Its shape was unmistakable – a very large male polar bear that had been seen over the past few days. The bear was clearly after the young geese. Des banged on the tent wall. The bear replied by ripping through it with his sharp claws. The unfamiliar feel and appearance of the tent may have scared the bear. In any event, after a few heart-stopping moments it loped off. Des afterwards said that it would not have been so bad if he had had some clothes on! After that the geese were kept in the scientists' hut.

Humans now intrude more and more on the Arctic. There are therefore bound to be more confrontations with bears. How many of these are genuine is a matter of concern. Anyone wishing to enhance his virility rating by shooting a polar bear can always insist the creature was killed in self-defence. The number of 'nuisance' bear-kills is steadily increasing. In the Northwest Territories of Canada there were 10 instances in 1977. Five years later the number had risen to 42. (These kills were in addition to the numbers eskimo settlements are allowed to take each year for legitimate hunting purposes.) That many of the bears are killed unnecessarily is almost beyond doubt – Dr Ian Stirling, a polar bear expert, has spent 20 years in the Arctic without once having to shoot a bear in self-defence.

The white coat is not only perfect camouflage out on the pack ice, it is also an important conductor of heat.

Government and industry have been working on ways of discouraging bears from annoying and frightening people, so that there is no excuse for shooting them. One relatively successful method involves punishing inquisitive bears with the equivalent of a plastic bullet. The selected bears are lured within range – 80 ft (24 m) – using drums of seal oil. The projectile does not do the animal any harm but does make it think that in future it might be better to steer clear of the area.

A face that knows and shows no fear simply because there are few creatures big, bold or strong enough to threaten its owner. Large bull walruses will sometimes face a polar bear and a defensive circle of musk oxen may persuade one to make a dignified retreat.

Despite these inevitable clashes between humans and polar bears, the overall position of this great carnivore is stable and possibly even improving. In 1973, the polar bear nations signed the Agreement on Conservation of Polar Bears. This made it illegal to hunt the bears on the high seas by plane or large motorised boats, also in areas where they had not previously been hunted by traditional means. The agreement requires that the countries concerned shall protect the eco-system, which places bears at the top of its food ladder. Denning and feeding areas are to be protected, as are migration routes. The signatory nations are to conduct and co-operate in research programmes, including marking and telemetry studies to learn more about bear movements. These movement studies have recently included the use of satellite tracking.

Much remains to be learned, but one of the early discoveries was that although polar bear migrations are highly complex there do exist more or less separate sub-populations. This enables the various nations to set reasonable hunting quotas within their own territories. Thus, Canada allows 600 bears to be killed annually, mostly by coastal eskimos. Among the total are around 15 bears that may be shot by licenced hunters, who are guided by eskimos. Alaskan eskimos are allowed around 100 bears a year. In Greenland, where the administration is shared by Denmark, eskimos may kill between 125 and 150 polar bears annually for subsistence and sale of skins. Norway stopped all hunting in the Svalbard island group because it judged that the bear population, which is shared with the USSR, was too low. Russia has banned all hunting since 1956.

Some say that the permitted annual kill is still too high for the world population of possibly 40,000 polar bears. The political issue concerning the hunting rights of native peoples, in this case the eskimos, is always problematic. The need to continue such hunting

Because of the size and nature of the bear's ice kingdom it is extremely hard to obtain an accurate estimate of the world population. It may be as high as 40,000. To study bear movements as a clue to population, radio transmitters are attached to darted bears. Signals are sometimes tracked by satellite.

Once a bear has been immobilised by darting, scientific measurements can be taken. The simplest method of weighing a polar bear is to attach bear and weighing scales to a helicopter.

is often questioned particularly as it is practised with sophisticated, high-powered rifles, where it was once carried out with traditional weapons such as the harpoon. Despite this, the international co-operation that has been achieved by the polar bear nations is held up, with some justice, as a model of international conservation. As has been pointed out previously, the predator is the most vulnerable of creatures since it depends on an intact eco-system for support. The Arctic Ocean is a particularly fragile eco-system which mankind can easily fracture.

Penguin Islands

G reat Britain does not possess a national park worthy of the name. But if it wants to create one, it need only look between latitudes 51° and 53° south, and longitudes 57.30° and 61.30° west where the Falkland Islands lie. Here, Britain could follow the example of Ecuador's protection of the Galapagos Islands and create a wildlife sanctuary.

The islands have a human population of approximately 2,000, against a wildlife population of many millions. They lie on the extension of the contintental shelf that reaches out from the Patagonian coast of South America. They are also approximately 310 miles (499 km) from the nearest part of the mainland of Tierra del Fuego, and some 800 miles (1,287 km) west of South Georgia. There are two main islands, East and West Falkland, separated by Falkland Sound. Two hundred smaller islands lie anything from 1 to 70 miles (1.6–112 km) offshore, mainly around West Falkland. Everything from the vegetation to the wildlife is governed by the surrounding cold seas, and almost all the Falkland wildlife depends for its livelihood on the fertile South Atlantic waters.

One of the first things you notice about the human males is that they continually blink. My own theory is that the men who work out in 'the camp' (Falkland for countryside, derived from the Spanish word *campo*) are so buffeted by the wind that their eyes continually water. Calm periods are rare, and usually occur in winter. The rest of the time the windspeed averages 15mph (24 km/ hr), reaching gale force on at least four days every month. Despite these conditions the temperature never drops very far. Snow is rare on the low ground and seldom lies for more than a few days. The

A pair of striated caracara, known in the Falklands as 'Johnny Rooks'. This handsome bird of prey is extremely curious and surprisingly tame. It feeds on chicks, eggs, carrion and will sample almost anything.

114

The Falklands consist of two main islands and 200 smaller ones, mainly around West Falkland. The pattern of islands and their landscape bear a strong resemblance to the less mountainous islands of Scotland.

humidity is high because of the oceanic situation, and there are few cloudless days. This pattern, with little seasonal variation, is precisely what you would expect on islands governed by a temperate ocean climate.

Climate and soil produce the Falklands' rather limited flora. Luckily, though, some of the islands' plants form a habitat that is ideal for the creatures that emerge from the sea to breed. Equally significant is the absence of native trees on the islands. The winds are too strong and the soil too acid to have encouraged their growth. However, trees have been introduced as wind-breaks around settlements, and they have had a hard struggle to survive, being mainly stunted. Gorse, planted for the same purpose, has fared much better.

The grassland which supports the sheep – always the islands' mainstay – is known as oceanic heath. Small areas of good quality meadow grass occur around some settlements, in valleys, close to the coast, and around the larger ponds. The 'hard camp' – Falklandese for the better drained areas – supports thick patches of a dark resinous shrub known as 'diddle-dee'. If these were Scottish islands, which in many ways the Falklands resemble, diddle-dee would be replaced by heather.

The native plant which is of most benefit to the island's wildlife is tussock-grass. Tussock, or tussac, grows to a height of 15 ft (4.5 m). It forms a fibrous pedestal about 3 ft (1 m) high. From the top grow long leaves and flower stems. When the leaves die down, they droop around the base, and new leaves sprout from the top. Dense strands of these leaves form an almost impenetrable tangle providing nesting cover for birds, and resting and pupping areas for fur and elephant seals. Tussock grass provides plenty of bird food, including beetles, spiders, and flightless crickets.

Comparatively little ornithological study has been carried out in the Falklands. However, a survey of one tussock island revealed that 5,000 pairs of 28 species were nesting there. Within the 13 ft (4 m) height to which it grows, tussock grass supplies an abundance and variety of habitat equal to that of a broadleaf woodland in a temperate climate where the trees stand up to 50 ft (15 m) high.

The second habitat which supports much of the Falklands fauna is found offshore in the giant kelp beds. The abundance of this algae can be gauged by the fact that the islands themselves are often known as kelpers. Although many of the beaches are either of white sand or arc boulder-strewn, neither of which are particularly rich in food, they do attract large numbers of birds.

Tussock grass is the most important plant for Falklands wildlife. It provides nesting cover for many species of birds and resting and calving grounds for elephant and fur seals.

The reason is that frequent storms tear great mats of giant kelp from the seabed and drive it onshore. There, piles of decaying algae support millions of fly larvae and harbour crustaceans on which shore and even land birds feed.

In his *Birds of the Falkland Islands* (1975), Robin W. Woods, the leading expert on the ornithology of the islands, lists 152 species. Of these, 66 have either bred or are thought to have bred, 13 are regular non-breeding visitors, and 73 are either vagrants or lost breeding species. The majority, 41 species, are closely related to, or indistinguishable from, South American breeding birds. Only one bird is recognised as unique to the islands, the Falkland flightless steamer duck, locally called the loggerhead or logger. It is a close relative of the flying steamer duck, also present in the islands as well as on the mainland. It is found along the shoreline.

The lack of disturbance and the homogeneous habitat means Falkland bird species are widely distributed throughout the islands. Some of the smaller islands are exceptional in the numbers of seabirds resident at nesting time. Two such islands are Beauchene, and Steeple Jason which lies 30 miles (48 km) north-west of West Falkland (both are uninhabited).

The Falklands' summer begins in September. This is when the first penguins return from their winter at sea to breed. They come battling ashore through the waves and over rocks. If a man tried to swim in such conditions he would probably never survive, but the penguins are protected by a thick layer of blubber and bounce off the rocks like rubber balls.

The flightless steamer duck is the only endemic Falklands species. There is also a slightly smaller flying steamer duck. The name comes from the way in which both 'steam' over the water, kicking up a great deal of spray and making a large bow wave.

Steeple Jason is approximately 7 miles (11 km) long, of which 6 miles (10 km) are occupied by birds during the breeding season. By the time they have all come ashore, or made their landing, there are 5 million birds along Steeple Jason's ridges and cliffs. One colony alone contains three million. Most are penguins, but there are at least 200,000 black-browed albatrosses among them, as well as several thousand rock and king shags.

The islanders used to keep sheep on Steeple Jason, but it was too remote and proved unprofitable. Now the grass is cropped by upland geese, one of the Falklands' four goose species. The others are the ashy-headed, ruddy-headed, and kelp goose (which feeds on algae along the shoreline). Sheep farmers have always seen the upland goose as a competitor for their grazing, and there was even once a bounty on this bird. It is still a valuable source of food, providing a change from mutton (Falklanders say that they eat mutton every day, reserving lamb for Christmas). Despite the

The kelp goose is without any doubt the most handsome of Falklands wildfowl. The male is totally white; the female, in the foreground, richly barred.

119

pressures on this handsome bird – the male is white and the female rufous-headed, with a barred chest – it continues to flourish.

Three of the Falkland's penguins – the magellan, gentoo, and rockhopper – nest on Steeple Jason. The fourth species is the king penguin (see Chapter Three). Kings had nearly been exterminated by the sealers in 1870, but a small colony has been preserved on East Falkland. The fifth species is the macaroni penguin, which greatly resembles the rockhopper. Since the macaroni is at the northern end of its breeding range only occasional pairs turn up. They seem to be accepted by the rockhoppers. The reason why large numbers of different penguin species can breed on one comparatively small island is that all three have different nesting site requirements.

Magellanic penguins, also known as 'jackass penguins' because of their loud braying call. They nest anywhere that they can dig a burrow.

Starting at the bottom, the magellan penguin is the only Falkland species that nests underground. It can be found almost anywhere that is suitable for burrowing. A favourite nesting place is at the base of a tussock clump. All penguins have a fairly discordant call, but magellans beat them all when it comes to cacophony. The local name both in the Falklands and on the South American mainland is jackass penguin. The bray is almost indistinguishable from that of a donkey. The birds belong to the family of black-footed penguins, and are easily distinguished from the rest by their black feet, their black and white faces, and neck bands. They have close relatives in Patagonia, Peru, the Galapagos, and South Africa.

The next species, the gentoo penguins, nest on level, open ground up to 1 mile (1.6 km) away from the sea. They choose shallow sandy beaches on which to make their landfall, and waddle overland to their nesting sites. They are big birds, next in size to

the king penguin, but are easily distinguished from all the other species by their white 'headscarves'. No one seems to be certain where the name gentoo comes from, but it was probably the nearest that sailors could once get to the Spanish *juanitos*, meaning little man. The penguins choose the same nesting grounds each year. Soon after their arrival they commence courting and establishing pair bonds. As with all penguins, this is a quarrelsome, raucous affair. Nest-building is extremely rudimentary, and consists of collecting a few stones, or stealing them from a neighbour, and presenting them to a partner.

The rockhoppers are by far the most numerous of the Falkland penguins and, from an observer's viewpoint are easily the most entertaining. Long ago the penguins discovered that if they could colonise parts of the island other penguins could not reach, they could enjoy nesting accommodation without competition for space.

In the Falklands, gentoo penguins, distinguished by their white 'head scarves', usually choose to nest on flat, open, grassy ground often a fair way from the sea. On Sub-Antarctic islands, such as South Georgia, they are often restricted to rocky surfaces like these.

121

The rockhoppers therefore developed a hopping method of locomotion that enabled them to scale or find ways around boulders and large rocks. Each jump is taken with both feet close together. Sharp nails in their toes provide the grip. On very steep slopes the birds use their beaks for added support. Rockhoppers have been doing this for so long that the rocky 'steps', by which the birds reach their clifftop nesting colonies, are often scarred and grooved by centuries of rockhopping. Some colonies are as much as 350 ft (106 m) above sea level. The only disadvantage of the system is that when one of the pair wishes to fish for krill or squid, it has to hop all the way back down again. But since the bird usually spends days and sometimes weeks at sea, this is not too high a price to pay for a good nesting site.

A rockhopper colony is seldom totally exclusive. Black-browed albatrosses and king cormorants often also share the ledges and clifftops, though this is not regarded by the penguins as unaccept-

This charming if dishevelled face belongs to a rockhopper penguin that has not yet attained the full glory of adult plumage with its handsome yellow head plumes.

This black-browed albatross is soaring around the nesting cliffs in the Falklands. On Beauchene, an uninhabited island 40 miles south of East Falkland, there is an albatross colony of gigantic size.

able competition. The only other penguin species that dares intrude on the rockhopper is the occasional pair of macaroni penguins. It is believed that the name Macaroni arose because the penguin's head of golden plumes – larger and more splendid than those of the rockhopper – resembles the eighteenth-century dandies who aped continental fashions. The line 'stuck a feather in his hat and called it macaroni' from *Yankee Doodle* may share a similar origin.

The albatross that shares the clifftops with the rockhoppers is probably the Falklands' most spectacular bird. All albatrosses take a great deal of time to rear their single young to the flying stage. They also court and build their conical mud nests before the penguins come ashore, and their young remain long after the penguins and their young have left. The breeding season for the black-browed albatross lasts from September until April.

Despite its 8 ft (2.4 m) wingspan, the black-browed albatross, with its snowy white head and black line to either side of the eye, is one of the smaller members of the family. Unlike the largest member, the wandering albatross – which visits the Falklands but does not breed there – the black-browed does not spend its sea life circumnavigating the Antarctic continent on the prevailing winds of the Southern Ocean. When it leaves after the breeding season it migrates north into the South Atlantic. It uses exactly the same flight techniques as the wanderer and the other members of the its family.

All albatrosses are built like high-performance sailplanes with extremely high-aspect ratio wings, that is to say great length combined with little breadth. They are light-boned, streamlined, and equipped with an undercarriage which gives far better service in the water when used for paddling, than when lowered for touching down or taking off on land.

Just as sailplanes can only operate efficiently where there are upcurrents and thermals, or rising masses of warm air, albatrosses can only put their aerodynamically excellent 'design' to best use where there are constant winds. The 'Roaring Forties' were not given this name lightly. Around latitude 40° south and below the winds blow more strongly than across any other ocean. And this is where the world's albatrosses – except for two North Pacific species – are found. (The black-browed, as already mentioned, operates to the north of the other southern species.) However, wherever an albatross is found it will use the same aerial technique – dynamic soaring.

It is best to view this from the stern of a ship. While it is possible that the albatross gains some advantage from the shelter, or even lift, that a moving ship provides, albatrosses progress by dynamic soaring whether there is a ship to help them or not.

The key factor is the friction between wind and sea surface. Because of this air-to-water friction, the windspeed is lower close to the surface of the ocean, especially in the troughs of the waves. Viewed from the after deck of a ship, the stages of dynamic soaring can be seen in sequence. The bird climbs to gain height against the headwind. It then begins a long shallow glide down into a wave trough. Because of the reduced air speed at that point its own speed quickens, so gaining distance. As its power begins to diminish, the albatross pulls up steeply and climbs to the height at which it began the manoeuvre and repeats the operation. Each time it does this it gains ground.

In the breeding season the albatrosses have little use for their flying skills, except when hunting food. In the nesting colony on top of the cliffs an albatross will lay its single egg. The rockhoppers all around will lay two. In fact penguins lay very large eggs, as do all birds whose young have to leave the nest soon after hatching. As soon as the second egg is laid the female starts incubating, but only for the first few hours, then the male takes over while she goes to sea to feed.

There are no mammal predators in the Falklands, except for bull sealions, who occasionally catch and eat penguins returning from fishing. The other marine mammals, the fur seals and the elephant seals, do not trouble the penguins. There are, however, many predatory or scavenging birds constantly hunting for unguarded eggs or chicks. Sheathbills, small pure white birds with pigeon-like movements and short, blunt powerful beaks are always searching

for unguarded eggs down on the shore. The caracaras, locally known as 'Johnny Rooks', are handsome, buzzard-like predators that never miss a chance to take an egg or unprotected chick. There are two species, the striated and the crested caracara. The name is an onomatopoeiac attempt to imitate the bird's harsh cries. Seizing young penguins is well within its capability. One day when watching magellan penguins in the tussock grass, I had my binoculars stolen by a caracara which flew 90 ft (27 m) with them before discovering they were inedible and dropping them to the ground. As an encore it stole a 35 mm film tin.

Two more scavenging birds include first the great skuas, villains the world over. The Falkland members of the clan frequently attack dogs and people who pass too close to their nests. Skuas take the eggs and young of all species. The final scavengers are the giant petrels, locally known as stinkers because of their ability to eject foul-smelling oil. Stinkers are the same size as the black-browed albatross, and will steal any available eggs and swallow sickly chicks. Fortunately seabird production is so abundant in the islands that predation makes no difference to the overall numbers. Predators, in all situations, exist in proportion to the food available to them.

How the bird got its name! Rockhoppers not only hop down but upwards to clifftop colonies that are sometimes 300 ft above the sea. Generations of rockhoppers' feet have often worn steps in the rocky paths.

When the first rockhopper chicks hatch, the male parent is usually still brooding the eggs. The birds returning from the sea, and sleek with good feeding, are therefore mostly females. Some have been away for up to three weeks. Perhaps the finest place to see this return from sea feeding is at the rockhopper colony on New Island, also off West Falkland, but closer inshore than Steeple Jason. Here you can survey the whole scene from the clifftop, hundreds of feet above the ocean. On reaching shore the rockhoppers swim and splash around playfully in a tidal pool at the foot of the cliff. Why they should want to do so after days, even weeks, at sea is impossible to tell. Possibly they enjoy the tranquillity of the pool after being buffeted about in the ocean. They take a short rest, particularly on sunny days, on the flat shelves around the pool and then begin the long climb to the nest to start cramming their newly hatched chicks with predigested sea food.

Rockhoppers going to sea in this colony sometimes have problems at low tide. There is a favourite launching point, like a miniature dock in the rock with sides that drop vertically 15 ft (4.5 m) to the water. At high tide jumping in presents no difficulties. At low tide, the birds wait for a big swell to come sweeping up the gulley, timing their jump as the water reaches

A mixed colony of black-browed albatrosses and king cormorants. The reddish colour of the pool is due to droppings of birds that have been feeding on marine organisms, mainly krill.

their position. Sometimes they get it wrong and drop straight into the trough to be thrown against the rocks by the next surge. This savage treatment does them no harm, and in fact they seem to enjoy it.

On a rich diet of seafood, the rockhopper chicks soon grow to resemble fluffy beachballs. In time they become so big that their parents cannot shelter them any longer. The chicks creep out and stand beside the adults.

The next stage involves the young penguins forming groups while both parents go fishing. This huddling together seems to provide them with sufficient protection from skuas and other raiders. The parents return frequently to feed their young. The final stage in the young rockhopper's development is to moult all its baby down in preparation for growing its sea-going feathers. Since a penguin has more feathers than any other bird, the colony soon resembles the scene of a gigantic pillow fight.

The parents now feed their young less regularly, so sharpening · their appetite, and encouraging them to feed themselves. The young are also beginning to resemble the adults. The golden 'eyebrows' are starting to sprout, although they will not reach their full glory for a year. The current batch of chicks venture closer to the sea, gradually moving down the steps in the rocks scarred and worn smooth by thousands of previous generations of rockhoppers. Sometimes the adults return to lead them, or provide a last feed on their way to their true home, the sea.

A South American tern colony in the tussock grass. In flight the slender wings and deeply forked tail with long streamers make the tern easily identifiable.

127

At this stage the parents need a good deal of food themselves. Once their young have safely launched themselves, they moult their own feathers. They could not afford to do so until this moment, having to be seaworthy to catch all the food needed to rear their offspring.

When moulting commences, the birds face two or three weeks of fasting. By the end of April, the colony is empty of young and old. All the rockhoppers are at sea, and they remain there until the following spring, which arrives in September.

However, the black-browed albatrosses have not yet left. Parents are still feeding their fully fledged young. The young albatrosses take their first flying lessons without actually leaving

The black-crowned night heron is the only resident heron of the Falklands, where locals call it the 'quark' after its raucous cry.

the ground, and need a good headwind to practise. They stand facing into the wind and flap their long wings, from time to time hopping awkwardly a few inches into the air. Some make a trial attempt down the rocky runway towards the cliff edge. They look so ungainly at this stage that it is hard to believe they will shortly become masters of the air. But soon, one dusk or early morning, when the winds off the sea are favourable, they will eventually launch themselves from the cliff edge, apparently with complete confidence, and effortlessly bank and soar down towards the ocean.

The young rockhoppers will not disappear from sight of land immediately. They will stay close inshore for a while, getting used to the surf and the big Atlantic swells, learning how to swim, dive, fly under water using their stubby flipper-like wings and, most important, discovering how to catch krill, squid and small fish. Next year they may return to the area where they were hatched, but they will not be able to breed until they are at least three. One or two bold rockhoppers may climb the rocky steps and approach the colony out of curiosity, but they will not dare enter. If they did, they would be attacked and driven off by the adults. So, they pass the time swimming and sunbathing, sensing that their time will come. Indeed there is no rush – penguins have a long natural life, perhaps as much as 25 or 30 years.

The future of the Falklands as an ocean sanctuary looks reasonably secure. Mercifully, the Falklands war did not greatly disturb or destroy wildlife. The conflict took place at a time when the great bird colonies were not occupied, and the penguins and albatrosses were still at sea. Yet there are threats ahead. It is possible that oil may be found between the islands and the mainland. Furthermore, since the war increasing numbers of European and Russian deep-water trawlers have been harvesting the rich hauls of fish in the South Atlantic. A severe drop in the penguin population a year or two after the war was attributed to overfishing, although the case against the trawler fleets remained unproven.

There is every sign that the Falkland islanders are proud of their immense seabird inheritance, and wish to protect it. But the future of the islands is by no means certain. Argentina seems highly unlikely to renounce her claim to the Falklands. Before there is any danger of further conflict, or perhaps even a compromise solution, it is up to Britain to guarantee for all time the security of the islands' magnificent wildlife.

Calm periods are rare. Gales occur about four days a month. Many windjammers damaged trying to round Cape Horn just made it north-east to the Falklands to die.

The Passing of Leviathan

In the Psalms the whale is described as 'That Leviathan whom God has made to take his pastime in the oceans. 'And in the story of the Creation is the account of God creating, great whales . . . and every living creature that moveth which the waters brought forth abundantly after their kind . . . And God saw that it was good and God blessed them saying: "Be fruitful and multiply and fill the waters in the sea." '

Modern science might not agree with all this, but it would confirm one point. The great whales and their lesser relatives, the dolphins, were fruitful and did multiply . . . until man came on the scene and all but hunted them from the kingdom of the deep.

The slaughter of the whale has taken place in a remarkably short timespan. It seems that the moment mankind finds the means, he uses it to destroy what might otherwise have been an infinitely renewable resource: the gun put an end to the buffalo of North America; and the chainsaw and axe are destroying the rain forests. In the case of the great whales, the fast steam whale catcher and the explosive-headed harpoon inflicted terrible damage.

Whaling, of course, started long before these weapons were found on ships. The Basques were probably the first to hunt whales. They pursued the Biscayan right whale about the time William of Normandy invaded England. In fact they were such successful hunters that they soon had to sail further afield. Without the benefit of compasses or navigating aids they sailed to Iceland, Spitsbergen, and Greenland. And, in 1614, the English and the Dutch even came close to fighting over who held the Spitsbergen whaling rights.

Fifty tonnes of southern right whale breaches, jumping clear of the water. It is thought that whales breach, particularly in rough weather, to let each other know where they are.

When whales were still abundant in Antarctic waters, these two catchers Diaz *and* Albatros *sailed out of South Georgia to reap the harvest. Now they lie derelict in the abandoned harbour at Grytviken, a monument to an industry that shot itself out of business.*

But the story does not finish there. The British had become concerned about the decline of the whales in southern waters and perhaps jealous of the Norwegians' success. In 1906 they introduced rules aimed at protecting the species around the islands they administered, including the Falklands and South Georgia. The Norwegians resented this interference and sought to avoid using British-owned bases, so evading their restrictions. The Norwegian alternative was the factory ship that enabled the whales to be processed at sea. Ironically, by setting up controls, the British had accelerated the decline of whale stocks. Between 1910 and 1940 the annual whale kill rose from 12,000 to 40,000.

Norway and Britain monopolised the Antarctic waters until 1934 when the Japanese joined the whale hunt. The Germans followed in 1935. After the Second World War the USSR, the USA and Australia went whaling in southern waters until, by the 1960s, history had once again been repeated. There were not enough great whales left in these waters to make the journey worthwhile. Japan then purchased the whaling fleets of the other nations, with the exception of the USSR. Because the Japanese have a great appetite for whale meat they continued the hunt, down to the smallest of the rorquals, the minke whale, of which there were, and are, still a considerable number. At present the Japanese have scaled down their activities for 'scientific study'. But whatever the purpose, the minkes still get killed and the meat is still served in Japanese restaurants.

The true tragedy lies in the fact that there is nothing extracted from the whale that cannot be obtained or manufactured by other means – except for the whale meat.

There are 10 species of great whale, and they include the southern and northern right whale, and the bowhead or Greenhead whale, limited numbers of which are permitted to be killed by eskimos each year. The right whales gained their name by virtue of the fact that they were slow swimmers, and therefore the right whales to hunt. Early hunters also preferred the right whales because their large quanties of blubber meant that they floated after death.

Right whales do not have a dorsal fin, unlike the fin whales. The latter include the blue whale – the largest animal the world has ever known – in addition the fin, sei, Bryde's whale, and the humpback (see Chapter Two). The smallest of the fins is the little minke whale, named after a Norwegian captain – Meincke – who exaggerated the size of his catch. A minke whale rarely measures more than 26 ft (8 m) long. All the fin whales are known as rorquals, the Norwegian word for 'grooved'. It refers to the pleats along the throat which expand to let the whales take in huge quantities of water when filtering out their staple diet of krill.

The sperm whale is perhaps the most impressive of the great whales, and the only one with teeth instead of baleen plates. The teeth are only in its narrow bottom jaw, and when the mouth is

Once one of the prime targets of the harpoon gunner; the tin whale is second only to the blue whale in size. A fin weighs up to 40 tonnes. Fortunately, the species is still fairly numerous.

closed they fit into recesses in the upper jaw. Moby Dick, the white whale obsessively hunted by Captain Ahab, was a sperm whale. All the other toothed cetaceans are dolphins, a term denoting the smaller members of the whale family.

The great whales are immense, warm-blooded, air-breathing, and highly remarkable animals whose appearance is confusingly similar. They are not easily identified by the casual observer, fortunate enough to see one from the deck of a ship. Like an iceberg, most of a surface-swimming whale is below the water line.

The right whale, whether of the northern or southern race, is a stubby creature averaging 49 ft (15 m) long, weighing approximately 50–55 tonnes. The back can be as much as 10 ft (3 m) wide. The head, with the huge mouth curved like a flamingo's beak, takes up a quarter of the length. The tail flukes are broad with pointed tips, and have a deep notch in the middle. One of the right whale's most peculiar features are the white patches, known as 'callosities'. Many people believe them to be barnacles; they are the whales' equivalent of facial hair, growing roughly where a man has eyebrows, moustache, and a beard. Roger Payne who studied the southern right whales in the Gulf of St Matias (near Peninsular Valdes, on the Patagonian coast) for several breeding seasons, was able to identify individual whales by the pattern of callosities. These never change and are as unique to a whale as finger prints are to a human.

It is also sometimes possible to identify the species of whale by the shape of its 'blow' – the exhalation of water vapour. The right whale's blowholes are placed in a V-shape, and the column of vapour tends to take the same shape. It is difficult, if not impossible, to estimate the numbers of any species left in the world's oceans. The current scientific estimate is that there are no more than 2,000 southern right whales, perhaps 200 of which breed and rear their young in the sheltered waters inside Peninsular Valdes.

Bowheads are very similar to right whales, but are even dumpier. Although they are also approximately 49 ft (15 m) long, they can weigh nearly twice as much – up to 90 tonnes. The head is also longer than in the right whale, while the jaws (which give them their name) are highly arched to house long curtains of baleen plates. It is alleged that two buses could pass through the arch of the jaws in opposite directions without touching. Bowheads do not have callosities. For political reasons Alaskan eskimos are allowed to kill a limited number of these whales, so preserving their hunting traditions. Many conservationists feel that this would be reasonable if they were compelled to hunt with the traditional weapon, the toggle-headed harpoon, instead of modern harpoon guns. Today, the world bowhead population is probably no more than 3,000.

The female blue whale averages 85 ft (26 m) in length, and a weight of 105 tonnes. The males are slightly smaller. It is said that a blue whale's arteries are so wide that a child could crawl through

Squid form part of the diet of many creatures, including the whale. Some surface from the depths of the sea at night, when they appear to glow in the dark. This shoal is travelling by means of water-jet propulsion.

them. The whale's body is streamlined and slatey blue in colour, with a small triangular fin set well at the rear. The blow is a single vertical column of vapour droplets that can reach 39 ft (12 m) high. The most extensive kill of blue whales occurred in the 1930s, after which the population has never recovered. One optimistic estimate puts the world total at 10,000, of which 7,000 are likely to be in the Antarctic.

Fin whales are a smaller version of the blue whale, weighing up to 40 tonnes. They have a very distinctive colour, being darker on the top half and lighter below. At the head this pattern interestingly takes a quarter turn to the left. Also, the blow is made at an angle rather than vertically. Fortunately fins are still numerous, and there are possibly as many as 75,000 left.

The right whale got its name because it was the right whale to hunt. When dead it tended to float rather than sink. The white 'growths' around the head are not barnacles but 'callosities', sensitive patches which the whale carries where a man would have hair.

Barnacles anchor themselves to whales, often among the callosities of right whales. These barnacles are attached to a gray whale. Among them parasites, such as the whale lice that can be seen here, find a living.

Sei whales are one size down from the fin, averaging around 12½ tonnes. The fin is larger than in the blue or fin whales, and is set much further forward. The word sei, or seje, is Norwegian for pollack, a fish of the cod family. The Norwegian whalers used this name because they appear off the Norwegian coast at the same time as the pollack shoals, presumably when the plankton on which both feed, begins to appear. Population estimates for sei whales are 80,000, and for Bryde's – the last of the fin whales and the smallest at 12 tonnes – 20,000. Although this sounds like a great many whales, spread over the huge oceans it means they are not always easy to find. Both need protection, almost as much as the more persecuted species.

The gray whale, the only member of the family *Eschritidae*, occurs between the right whales and the rorquals. They are perhaps the least attractive looking of all the great whales, being coloured blotchy grey, with tattered looking tail flukes. Instead of a fin they have 7–10 knobs along their rear dorsal surface.

139

Gray whales have strange feeding habits. They take in giant kelp, strip it of any animal food found in the fronds, and then eject it uneaten. Underwater photography has also revealed 'mouth prints' on the sandy sea bed, where the whales have apparently stood on their heads taking in bottom silt, sifting it for animal organisms. The grays are confined to the eastern Pacific, and migrate between the Gulf of California and the Arctic. They travel close to the coast and are therefore easy to catch. Not so long ago many gray whales ended up in Mexican dog food factories. Now, with full protection, their numbers are building up, and there are probably 15,000 left. They can grow to 50 ft (15 m) length, and weigh up to 35 tonnes.

There is no mistaking the sperm whale when it breaches or leaps out of the water, revealing its immense, blunt head. It is an extraordinary sight. Sperms differ from the other great whales in many ways. They are the only species in which the male is usually bigger than the female. And, they appear to have a different social system, the big males herding harems of up to 30 females. These big bulls can grow to 60 ft (18 m) long, and weigh up to 50 tonnes.

Sperm whales feed largely on giant squid which they hunt at immense depths. They are known to feed in the total darkness of the ocean 3,000 ft (914 m) below the surface. Eyesight certainly cannot be used when feeding in the blackness of the benthos, the coldest darkest realm in the kingdom of the deep. The whales probably locate their prey by echo-location.

The sperm whales continuously emit a series of powerful clicking sounds. It has been said that listening to a herd of sperm whales is like hearing an army of carpenters hammering nails into a wall. It is highly likely that echoes from these monotonous clicks provide the whale with a 'sound picture' of the ocean bottom, and indicate the presence of prey. That titanic battles occur in the dark depths between sperm whales and giant squid is clear from the sucker marks sometimes found on whales' bodies. They indicate that some of the squid, fighting to escape the most massive teeth in the world, must have had tentacles up to 18 ft (5 m) long.

Although the whale's immense, blunt head contains the largest brain of any creature that has ever lived, it does not necessarily indicate great intelligence. In fact quite a small brain can control the functions of an enormous body, as the dinosaurs successfully demonstrated. However, much of the sperm whale's brain is highly developed, like a human's. What it uses this for, unless it is echo-location, no one knows. Nor can science yet answer how the sperm whale's body withstands the tremendous water pressures encountered at such enormous depths.

The huge head contains another mysterious organ, and one that played a large part in the animal's destruction – a reservoir of the finest natural oil in the world, known as spermaceti wax. This wax acts as a buoyancy chamber, possibly also an aid to echo-location. The density of this normally liquid wax depends on temperature. It

A gray whale lolls on the surface, rolling half on its side. One flipper is nearly out of the water. One eye can be seen as well as a large group of barnacles on the upper jaw.

seems likely that the whale can adjust its buoyancy, allowing water to cool the wax by flooding its right nasal passage which runs through the spermaceti. Since this passage is 3 ft (1 m) wide and 5.5 ft (5 m) long, cold water can easily solidify part or all of the wax, also reducing buoyancy. Warming the wax makes it expand as it becomes liquid and so its density drops. Cooling it leads to contraction as it solidifies into a wax and its density rises.

The unconfirmed record dive involves two male sperm males killed off the coast at Durban. They were harpooned after an 80-minute dive. In their stomachs were sharks known to live only at the bottom of the sea, 9,500 ft (2,895 m) down.

Although many fascinating discoveries have been made about whales in the last 25 years, they remain the hardest of all marine creatures to study because of their size, wide distribution, and general inaccessibility. However, scientists, including Hal White-head of Britain (who has sailed the world in his own yacht studying

141

sperm whales) and Roger Payne (who has researched off Bermuda, Hawaii, and Patagonia into humpback and right whale behaviour), have added greatly to our knowledge. Perhaps the best summary of their findings, and history of the whale and whaling, is to be found in the excellent *The Hunting of the Whale*, by Jeremy Cherfas.

I myself learned much about the southern right whale when working with Roger Payne on a Survival documentary. In particular I discovered that in rough weather whales probably communicate with each other by breaching, leaping clear of the water and crashing back. It is hard to imagine the power that those tail flukes must generate to hurl 50 tonnes of whale clear of the water. Whales also communicate their whereabouts by the technique of lob-tailing, which involves slapping the surface repeatedly with their tails, making a noise like cannon shots.

A sperm whale breaching. The sperm whale has the largest brain of any animal in the world. Much of the brain is probably concerned with echo-location as a means of finding its prey.

It was a revelation to me that whales sail by standing on their heads in the water, allowing the wind to catch their tail flukes so blowing them along. I also discovered that whales can get sunburnt when lying with their backs exposed. Gulls perch on the whales' backs stripping off the peeling skin which is, surprisingly, paper-thin. Another surprising fact is that whales are not aggressive when approached respectfully in a rubber boat. Several miles off the Alaskan coast I have sat in a zodiak with humpback whales rolling and blowing so close that the noise was deafening, and the distinctly fishy smelling spray soaked my companions and myself. The whales repeated the performance so often that it was hard not to think that they were also enjoying the encounter.

A stranded sperm whale dies. It is quite unlike any other great whale, being toothed. The holding teeth in the long, thin lower jaw fit into recesses in the upper jaw. The huge blunt head gives it a strange unbalanced appearance.

But do the great whales have a future? Despite the tremendous amount of public support for their conservation it is hard to be optimistic. If a moratorium on all whale-hunting could be declared at this moment and remain in force for the next 50 years, then there might be a chance for the more endangered species. Even so it may be too late for some species, notably the sperm whale, whose social structure may well have been irrevocably destroyed. Male sperm whales need to be 25 years old before they can command a harem for breeding purposes. Even if catching stopped immediately it would be a long time before the world population began to fulfil its breeding potential.

Flensing knives make short work of cutting through blubber and whale meat on the factory ship's slipway. Although factory ships have been phased out for hunting the great whales, an unjustifiable number of the smaller minke whales are still caught.

The International Whaling Commission was established in 1946 by 14 whaling nations to set catching quotas, and to regulate the harvesting of whales. While it has had some partial successes, there have been more partial or total set-backs. The commission has often been dismissively referred to as a 'club for whalers'. Certainly, it has often looked like that, and it is hard for it to appear otherwise when the nations still interested in whaling govern its affairs. Nonetheless it came close to achieving a temporary moratorium on commercial whaling in 1979. But while it banned the use of factory fleets for processing larger wheels, it excluded minke whales, the only species still being caught in commercial numbers. This has been typical of the commission, mixing high hopes with dismay. The net result is always that nations wishing to continue whaling will always get their way.

In the unlikely event of there ever being a total ban on whaling, agreed by the member nations of the IWC, there remains the problem of the whaling nations outside the commission. They could easily purchase rusting and aged whaling ships, and use them to hunt whales as long as the ships operate and there is a profit to be made. It seems that the most powerful weapons to be used for whale conservation are economic and political, including bans on the import of fish products from those countries that refuse to save the whale. But this policy is not easy to operate, and can result in rival bans which create further economic difficulties.

The story of the three gray whales which become trapped in the ice, just off Barrow, the most northerly town in Alaska, in October 1989 seems to sum up the illogicalities, emotions, heroics and absurdities that surround the whole question of whales and whaling.

The whales had delayed their southward migration so long that they were caught in the fast ice of the Beaufort Sea. An eskimo hunter, Roy Ahmaogak, discovered their plight. Within one week they were headline news. Oil companies offered an ice-breaking barge, and two Sikorsky skycranes, the world's largest helicopters,

Compare this whale jaw with that of the dead sperm whale on the previous page. The southern right whale is a baleen whale that filters out its prey – krill or small fish – from hundreds of gallons of water by means of baleen or whalebone plates. These are seen clearly below the whale's upper jaw.

Efforts are made to release the gray whales caught in the ice near Barrow, Alaska.

tried to tow it 800 miles (1,287 km) to Barrow. But in one week they covered just 8 miles (12 km). A fortnight after their discovery, the whales were still stuck fast and obviously weakening. An Archimedean screw tractor was flown in by the US army in a C-5A, the largest aircraft in the world. And a seven-tonne spiked concrete yo-yo was dropped from a helicopter to smash the ice. Both methods worked – until the ice quickly refroze.

With time running out, the local eskimos moved in with chain saws and the hoe-shaped tools they themselves use when hunting bowhead whales. Having cut blocks of ice with the saws, they pushed them under the ice sheet and cleared two holes at intervals of 100 yds (91 km) from where the whales were trapped. Gradually they persuaded the whales to swim to the new holes. In this way they hoped to tempt them towards the open water which at one stage was just 3 miles (5 km) away.

At this point the Soviet Union agreed to divert two huge ice-breakers that were returning home to Vladivostok after six months at sea. As the ice-breakers smashed their way towards Barrow, the eskimos continued to tempt the whales by cutting new breathing holes. Sadly, Kannick, the smallest of the whales died. The two larger survivors reached the 25th hole and then refused to go any further. Sonar revealed that they were refusing to cross a ridge on the seabed. When a new pathway of holes was cut the whales immediately co-operated. Finally, the two 13,500 tonne ice-breakers, the *Vladimir Arseniev* and the *Admiral Makarov*, broke through the last obstruction, a pressure ridge in the ice 60 ft (18 m) thick, and opened a channel to unfrozen water.

Twenty one days after being spotted, the whales surfaced for the last time and escaped into open water.

The rescue had cost an estimated $1.3 million. No one will ever know whether the two surviving gray whales made it back to California. Ironically the Russians, who had played such a valuable part in the rescue, are permitted by the International Whaling Commission to kill 179 gray whales to feed eskimos on the Soviet side of the Bering Sea. And, on the very day the Americans asked Russia for help the American senate passed legislation that empowered the president to impose tougher sanctions on nations that defied whale conservation agreements. One week later, congress overturned the new measures.

The Duke of Edinburgh called the whale rescue 'a circus that would not have made a blind bit of difference' to whale conservation. And in a sense he was absolutely right. As he would probably admit, however, he overlooked the propaganda value of the enterprise in enlisting public support that can, and occasionally does, influence governments.

One final point needs to be made. The ice-breakers eventually set the whales free with the efforts and local knowledge of the eskimos or Inupiat, the People of the Whale. Ironically, the Inupiat are themselves whale hunters.

Search for the *Shinohara*

E ven by modern standards *Shinohara* was a big submarine. The I.169, the pride of the Japanese Imperial Navy, was launched at the Mitsubishi shipyard in Kobe on 28 September 1935. Submerged, she displaced 2,440 tonnes and her twin diesels could drive her at 23 knots on the surface so that she could, if necessary, operate with a battle fleet.

Her armament consisted of six bow and four stern torpedo tubes. Mounted on deck was a dual purpose 4 in (100 mm) gun for surface or anti-aircraft fighting, and two 13 mm anti-aircraft machine-guns. At an average surface speed of 10 knots she had a cruising range of 14,000 nautical miles (26,000 km).

When the Japanese launched their surprise attack on Pearl Harbor, the I.169 was on patrol in Hawaiian waters with the Third Submarine Flotilla. A few days after the attack, when lying on the surface at midnight, her crew witnessed the glare and noise of distant explosions as the American anti-submarine patrols exacted revenge for Pearl Harbor. Several members of her own flotilla had been detected and destroyed. The I.169 submerged and moved in closer to the devastated American fleet anchorage. Shortly afterwards she became entangled in the cables of anti-submarine defences and was trapped for 50 hours. Eventually she broke free without being detected, and returned to her operational base at Kwajalein Island.

At the crucial battle of Midway in the Pacific, the carrier action that altered the balance of power against the Japanese, the *Shinohara* was on patrol with the Twelfth Submarine Squadron, hoping to intercept and shadow the American carrier fleet. But she

A crown of thorns starfish moves over a reef, killing and eating the coral polyps. Ten years ago it was feared that the starfish would wipe out Australia's Barrier Reef. The plague now seems to be dying out although 28 per cent of the reef has been damaged.

never made contact with them. Instead, she served as a commerce raider off the Australian coast where she sank some 20 cargo ships. Then, in February 1943, she was sent to patrol the foggy waters around the Aleutian Islands in the North Pacific, where she was at a considerable disadvantage. The American navy had radar, invaluable in poor visibility, which the Japanese still lacked. When the Americans reoccupied the island of Attu and the Japanese evacuated Kiska, she returned south to operate around the Solomons and off New Guinea. The Americans were now island-hopping to victory in the Pacific in one of the hardest fought and most difficult amphibious operations of World War Two. When they launched the invasion of the Gilbert Islands the Japanese ordered all submarines in that part of the Pacific to concentrate around this archipelago.

Fifty years later, the shores of Truk Lagoon are littered with the wrecks left by American air attacks on the Japanese naval base. Most of the wreckage lies on the seabed of the lagoon where the corals are taking over the sunken war and supply ships.

In April 1944, the *Shinohara* was based at Truk Lagoon in the Caroline Islands, the Japanese navy's advanced naval base in the Pacific. Her role was no longer sinking enemy ships but running supplies to the hard-pressed Japanese defenders on Rabaul. At dawn on 4 April, American carrier-based aircraft launched an all-out attack on Truk. The *Shinohara* was lying on the surface with four other boats of her flotilla. To escape the fate of the surrounding surface ships she dived immediately in 160 ft (48 m) of water, which was more than adequate to protect her from aerial bombing.

In the panic of the dive crewmen failed to close the valve on the torpedo loading hatch. Water flooded the torpedo area, but the crew managed to close water-tight doors and they should have been safe in the unflooded sections of the boat.

The aerial attack continued for three days, the American planes refuelling and re-arming immediately on returning to their carriers.

By the time land-based four-engined Liberators came in on the third day to finish off any boats still afloat, over 50 Japanese ships had been sunk and 148 Japanese fighters and bombers destroyed.

Truk had become Japan's Pearl Harbor. The few ships that escaped included all but one of the submarines. When the surviving submarines headed for the open sea, the *Shinohara* was not among them. Her oxygen supplies were now fast running out. All attempts to rescue her and the trapped crew failed. Thirteen bodies were later recovered but 84 men died inside her. The bottom of the 40 mile (64 km) anchorage of Truk was littered with wrecks, 80 war and supply ships, and an unknown number of fighters and bombers, few of them American.

The Micronesian authorities who administer the islands under American supervision today look upon Truk Lagoon as a monument to a terrible catastrophe. The position of all the main wrecks is known and charted, and each is regarded as a war grave. Only one was missing from the roll call – until very recently – and that was the I.169, the *Shinohara*.

Today fish live, feed and breed between the decks of the vessels, amongst the giant shells intended for the Japanese battleships, inside the tanks and trucks they were carrying as cargo. Wrecks anywhere are welcomed and quickly adopted by all manner of sea

The sea has laid its own flowers on the graves of Japanese sailors. Among a golden sunburst of Tubestrea aurea, *a small reef fish seeks a refuge from predators.*

151

Corals take many forms and shapes depending on water temperatures, depth and light. Many have names descriptive of their shapes. This diver is setting up lights to take pictures of 'dead man's fingers', more scientifically known as Alcyonium digitatum.

creatures. But in tropical seas there is one small animal above all that quickly attaches itself to any wreck it can find, provided it does not lie too deeply. In doing so it soon transforms the huge derelicts into a sea community of great beauty filled with life. The coral polyps drifting in the plankton swarms anchor themselves to the clean metal surface of sunken ships. They have become living and colourful instances of the ocean's ability to create life. They have become coral reefs.

Corals begin life as free-swimming, or rather drifting, specks of life called planulae. Countless billions of them drift in the plankton swarms. When one finds an anchor, a rock, a dead mass of coral, or a shipwreck, it attaches itself to the surface and becomes a fully fledged coral polyp. The word comes from the Greek, meaning 'many-footed'.

The coral polyp is another animal, like the shark and the crocodile, that got its design right almost from the beginning. The polyp, however, is much older than the other two, having existed for approximately 400 million years.

Coral polyps do not look very impressive, and despite the name, have no feet at all. The polyp consists of a fleshy sac with a mouth at the top, and a ring of tiny tentacles for clinging on to whatever anchor it eventually settles upon. It is such a vulnerable creature that it needs to build itself a small fortress. This is achieved by extracting calcium carbonate from the sea water. Once this mini castle has been erected, the polyp can retreat inside if danger threatens. The building process continues throughout the polyp's life, so that both the height and thickness of the limestone castle continually increases, raising the polyp within higher and higher. Soon the original colonist splits into two polyps, then two into four, and so on. In this way a colony is created.

As the colonies grow, their limestone secretions take many different shapes – plates, lobes, branches and towers. Different varieties of coral produce widely different limestone formations. The names of many reveal their shapes: staghorn coral, brain coral, elkhorn coral, fire coral (which stings), pillar coral, and so on. In a few years the original single polyp may have started a colony numbering tens of thousands of its descendants. None of these can move around, although a few predatory corals can reach out of their cases sufficiently far to devour their neighbours. Otherwise, they are stuck inside their limestone castles for life. But like many other sedentary marine creatures they take their food from the endless conveyer belt of the currents that bring the small organisms on which they feed right to their doorstep.

Reef-building corals can only exist in waters whose temperature does not fall below 23°C (72°F). Nor must it become too warm for them. This water is usually very clear, which means it is not loaded with nutrients or swarms of planktonic creatures. Nevertheless the polyps find sufficient to feed on, and collect the massive amount of material needed to build their limestone fortresses.

As colourful as any coral or reef fish but in fact a nudibranch, otherwise known as a sea slug. One of the most brilliant is known as 'The Spanish Dancer'. The type pictured here is a 'Spanish Shawl'.

Amazingly, two thirds of the living matter on a reef consists of plant tissue in the form of algae. Some of the algae live inside the polyps' bodies, others, even more mysteriously, inside the limestone cases where no light can reach them to assist in the process of photosynthesis essential to all plants. Scientists are uncertain whether these algae are parasites or whether they have a symbiotic relationship with the polyps, both parties benefiting from the partnership. It is even likely that the algae contribute to the limestone forming process.

The final stage in the development of a coral community is the reef. A single reef will contain thousands upon thousands of colonies. It can, like Australia's Great Barrier Reef, stretch for more than 1,000 miles (1,609 km). Competition for space on a reef is intense. One type of coral overgrows another, killing off its less successful neighbour. When this happens, the loser's skeleton remains in the form of a block of inanimate limestone which is promptly colonised by the victor. Only the surface of a coral formation is alive, as this is where the polyps exist. Beneath is a block of dead limestone as much as 1,000 ft (304 m) thick, built and abandoned by thousands, perhaps millions, of years of preceding polyp colonies. It is this limestock block, the reef, that has ripped the bottom out of countless ships.

The Greeks thought corals were the seeds of seaweed, distributed by the gorgon Medusa, whose look turned everyone to stone. Even Linnaeus, the eighteenth-century Swedish scientist (who invented a scientific system of naming flora and fauna that survives to this day), thought that corals were a sort of halfway house between animals and plants. In 1726, the French naturalist Jean André Peyssonnel showed that the sea's stone forests were built by animals. Typically, the eminent scientific bodies of the day refused to accept his theory. Even when the Royal Society of London published his work 30 years later, it did so anonymously.

The confusion was certainly understandable. Many of the most beautiful soft corals, the sea fans and the gorgonians, do look extraordinarily like plants as their 'leaves' and branches sway to the movement of undersea currents. And the skeletons of the much sought-after black and red gem corals, which are found at greater depths than the reef corals, bear a marked resemblance to twigs. Today Peyssonnel's detractors might take consolation from the thought that, as we now know, minute plants share the coral polyp's life intimately and are an important part of it, though we are still uncertain how and why.

The American diving team that set out for Truk in 1973 to find the *Shinohara* was lead by Al Giddings, one of the world's most

A sea urchin crawls over the base of a sea fan, or gorgonian, named after the creature in Greek mythology whose look turned people to stone. It has a skeleton of horny material supporting a colony of millions of polyps.

Giddings and the team were able to open a hatch and venture inside the doomed boat. They found the bones of crewmen on top of the diesels, the last place where they were able to find oxygen. They spent five minutes inside the submarine and then closed the hatch again.

When they told the Japanese government of their find, the Welfare Ministry allotted a budget of 34 million yen to salvage the remains of the crew and bring them back to Japan. When the salvage operation began next August, Japanese, American and Micronesian divers shared the work. Relatives were flown to Truk to take the ashes of their war dead back to Japan. Then the Japanese divers performed one final rite. They made one last dive

When the contents of the Shinohara *had been salvaged, the hatches were welded shut to that she would rest un-disturbed as a war grave. The Japanese government flew relatives of the dead sailors to Truk. A Shinto ceremony was held and the ashes taken back to Japan.*

to weld up the hatches for ever. The corals that were sprouting from her hull and had already taken over the stay of her radio antenna would be left to do the job of cementing the hatches even more firmly.

The Japanese have long experience of the value of sunken ships in producing artificial coral reefs. As long ago as the early eighteenth century they were deliberately scuttling old ships to encourage coral growth and improve inshore fishing. Coral reefs are a vital part of the eco-system in shallow tropical waters. They are important nurseries for the young of many commercial food and sport fish. These days, the latter bring revenue to many countries by attracting anglers and tourists. The reefs themselves are a magnet for skin divers. Along many coasts, coral reefs protect the shoreline against wave action, though they themselves often take the brunt of hurricane-force winds and sustain considerable damage. And, as in the rain forests, current research continually reveals new medical uses for compounds contained in reef species. There is, therefore, every reason to protect and encourage coral growth whenever possible.

In recent years there was justified widespread fear that the large starfish, known as the crown of thorns, was destroying vast areas of coral by eating the polyps, notably along Australia's Great Barrier Reef. Where the crown of thorns had fed, the coral was dead and only the bleached, white limestone remained. There seems no doubt that population explosions of crown of thorns starfish have taken place many times in the history of the tropical seas. The raiders have come and gone. The coral has regenerated and the situation has returned to normal. The damage caused has, in other words, been natural. Now, alas, most of the damage caused to coral throughout the tropics is no longer natural. It is caused by humans.

What the human race is doing to the coral reefs is only too well illustrated by what has happened in the Philippines, though the same could be said of Hawaii, Panama, and even Florida, in fact anywhere in the tropics where so called development (or exploitation), is taking place.

The Philippines have 7,000 islands, 11,185 miles (18,000 km) of coastline and 44,00 sq miles (113,960 km^2) of coral reef, to a depth of 262 ft (80 m). The human population is around 50 million and increasing at about the rate of 4 per cent per year. Of that population 87 per cent lives within 31 miles (50 km) of the sea. The human influence on the sea is clear from a survey by the Marine Sciences Centre in the late 1970s, which revealed that more than half the reefs were in a stage of 'progressive destruction'. Only 5 per cent were still in excellent condition. And those closest to big cities were the most damaged. So what are the causes of the decline?

The answers apply not only to the Philippines, but to every tropical ocean.

Reefs and their inhabitants, such as this soft coral, are at their most brilliantly coloured at night. Coral polyps retire inside their tiny limestone castles during the day and come out to feed and reveal their colours after dark.

The most serious causes of the decline are sedimentation, harmful fishing methods, and direct exploitation of the coral itself for souvenirs and, in the case of the large corals, for building material. By far the worst of these factors is sedimentation. Coral polyps cannot live when covered by silt.

Sedimentation in the Philippines comes mainly from poor land management, and bad agricultural and forestry practices which wash topsoil into the sea, choking the reefs. Other causes of sedimentation are more direct. Exploitation or destruction of mangroves, muck-shifting for building or oil drilling, and the dumping of mine tailings and effluents, including destructive chemicals. If any or all of these factors do not kill directly by smothering the polyps, they make the water so murky that sunlight cannot penetrate. The algae that live in mysterious association with the polyps can no longer photosynthesise, and the growth of the coral slows. The deeper reefs on the limits of light penetration are the ones that suffer most in this way.

Direct assaults on the coral are many: illegal use of dynamite to stun fish; use of traditional Japanese methods such as *kayakas* fishing (banging the bottom with poles) and *muro-ami* fishing (hitting the reef with rocks). Both are attempts to scare the fish out of hiding, and smash large areas of coral. Gathering small fish for the bait and aquarium trade involves breaking off sections of branched corals. These are then shaken in the boat to dislodge the small fish hidden in them. The aquarium trade concentrates on cleaner wrasse, little fish that occupy 'cleaning stations' in the reefs where big fish, such as groupers, come to be cleansed of parasites by them. The wrasse have an important part to play in the community of the reef but are caught in large numbers and sold.

Indiscriminate spearfishing depletes reefs everywhere of their bigger denizens, such as groupers and parrotfish. Anchors used by the increasing numbers of sport and inshore commercial fishermen destroy sizeable areas of coral. Corals to supply the tourist and souvenir trade are mainly the smaller branching types that provide homes for small fish and invertebrates. The Philippines has long been one of the major exporters of such corals, although it is by no means the only country that is guilty. About 60 per cent goes to America, and the rest to Japan and Europe. A reef that has been blasted with dynamite takes at least 30 years to recover half its area of live coral. Reefs damaged by some of the other fishing methods described probably take half as long.

In the late 1970s ex-President Marcos of the Philippines made a decree prohibiting the gathering or export of corals. But three years later the trade was still flourishing. The size and scope of the coral trade makes it difficult, if not impossible, to end it, particularly in a country where bribery among officials is ever-

Marine environmentalists concerned about the damage being done to coral reefs throughout the tropical seas have started to create artificial reefs by giving the polyps something like these concrete blocks to cling on to.

It may not look like it, but this is a coral reef in the making. Old motor tyres chained together make an ideal material for artificial reef formation.

present. A total ban on coral exploitation throughout the coral-growing countries is the only answer, but it is one not likely to be given in nations where so many people live at subsistence level and make their living from the trade. The solution, as in so many departments of conservation, is to manage the coral harvest in such a way that locals can benefit until alternative ways of earning a living can be found. But that is no easy task.

Reefs are being destroyed at such a rate that the creation of artificial ones is becoming a priority. A good deal of successful experimental work has been done around the coasts of America. In Florida, the depletion of reefs had seriously begun to affect the important spiny lobster fishing industry. Spiny lobsters, known in Britain as crayfish, need the shelter of holes and crannies which a reef provides. So breeze blocks wired together in batches were sunk to form the base of a new reef. The holes in the blocks provided the lobsters with hiding places from their enemies. Within two years the blocks were covered with sponges, algae, seasquirts, and the first soft corals.

On the west coast of America, old cars and truck bodies were sunk to form the skeleton of a new reef after the petrol and oil had been drained out of them. The ideal artificial reef material turned out to be another automotive waste product. Every year American motorists junk over 200 million worn-out tyres. The tyres were first slashed then pressed into weighted bales to prevent them floating. Tyre merchants were actually willing to pay to get rid of mounds of

unwanted tyres. The prize example is Montgomery Reef, off the Florida coast, near Fort Lauderdale. It consists of 2 million tyres, sunk in clumps rather than one unbroken mass because reef fishes prefer the edges instead of the middle of a reef.

Another type of artificial reef is being developed by the United States Geological Survey. This consists of rounded concrete domes, like giant lumps of brain coral. The difference is that each dome bears a few transplanted colonies of different corals in an attempt to get corals to grow in suitable waters where they have previously been unknown.

Until recently, the phrase 'reef-building animals' meant the tiny coral polyps that build their limestone castles in warm seas. Now its meaning must be extended to those conservationists who are trying to make good human damage. Let us hope that it is not already too late.

They look like tiny bottles but are, in fact, the tips of an anenome's tentacles, armed with stinging cells. They, too, benefit from the artificial reefs. Some reef denizens, including clown fish, have found a way of living among the poisonous tentacles without being fatally stung.

Killer Whale

Among the coastal Indians of the Pacific Northwest lived a mighty hunter whose name was Naatslanei. He hunted the seal and the walrus and the bowhead whale from his kayak and, like many hunters, he respected and identified with the sea creatures he often risked his life to kill.

Naatslanei liked to hunt with his three brothers-in-law, but they resented his skills for he was the most successful hunter of his tribe. So one day they marooned him on a rock that was covered at high tide and left him to drown. The youngest of the three did not want to leave him and pleaded with the others to relent, but they overpowered the young man and left Naatslanei to his fate.

In time a loon, a black and white water bird (or northern diver), came to Naatslanei's rescue, and took him to a secret world inside the rock. The people who lived in this magic kingdom placed him in a bubble in which he drifted safely ashore. Now the hunter sent for his wife, and told her to bring his tools to him secretly. He carved a terrible black and white monster which he called Keet. He told Keet that he had carved him to avenge a wrong. 'Kill my two eldest brothers-in-law, but spare the youngest'. Keet surprised the three brothers in their boat one day. He drowned the two eldest as instructed, and told the youngest to climb on his back so that he could carry him safely ashore.

Naatslanei commended Keet and told him that he was never to harm anyone again. Then he freed him into the sea. Keet was the name by which the tribe knew the killer whale. So far Keet has obeyed the order given to him. Although the killer whale is relentless in pursuit of the mammals that live in the sea there is no

The face of a killer, but not a killer of human beings. So far there is no record of a killer whale having made a lethal attack on a swimmer. They are, however, one of the oceans' most successful predators. A pod, or shoal, has even been seen to attack a blue whale.

authenticated record of his species ever having aggressively attacked a human being.

The Romans called the killer whale Orca, the demon from hell. Its scientific name is *Orcinus orca*, although it is often called orca by modern naturalists who wish to avoid the stigma attached to the word killer. But a killer it most certainly is. While it feeds largely on fish and squid, seabirds and even turtles, it is an opportunist feeder often taking larger prey. Orca will kill and eat seals,

The coastal Indians of the Pacific Northwest not only revered the killer whale but wove tribal legends around it. The killer whale is even celebrated on the tribe's totem poles.

sealions, and young elephant seals. Packs of killer whales, known as pods, will even attack large whales. One such attack has been filmed in the Sea of Cortez, the long gulf which lies between the peninsular of Baja California and the main part of Mexico.

If you wished to draw a dividing line between whales and dolphins, the killer whale would be good a point as any to start. Dolphins are really small whales, and porpoises even smaller ones. All are cetaceans, warm-blooded, air-breathing mammals. The one common characteristic shared by all dolphins is that they have conical teeth for seizing and holding prey. Although the sperm whale also has them, its sheer size makes it a whale beyond any shadow of doubt. Cetologists (whale experts) and taxonomists (those who scientifically classify fauna) still have to resolve exactly which of the smaller whales, or rather dolphins, is most closely related to which. But what is certain is that the dolphins, the *Delphinidae*, form by far the largest family of cetaceans. There are at least 30, and possibly as many as 50. Although the killer whale is technically a dolphin, it is practically the size of the minke whale, the smallest of the rorquals. Male killer whales reach a maximum length of 31½ ft (9.6 m), slightly longer than the minke but, at nine tonnes, weigh one tonne less.

Killer whales are nearly unmistakable. Confusion could only arise because other dolphins have the distinctive black and white markings of orca, although not in the same places or proportions. Hector's dolphin, only likely to be seen in New Zealand waters, is one example. But the killer whale's sheer size, as well as its liking for roving the oceans in herds, make it in this sense easy to identify. Groups vary from 2 or 3, up to 25 members or more, although exceptions do occur – in Icelandic waters several thousand whales have been reported in the same area.

When viewed at close range the killer whale cannot be mistaken. The body is long, thick, and streamlined, predominantly coloured jet black. On the underside it is pure white from the lower jaw to the flippers, the white area narrowing as its reached the anus. Afterwards, it widens out, rising in separate patches towards the tail. On either side of the head there is a white patch starting above the eye, finishing at a point level with the start of the flippers.

Males are bigger than females and they have one outstanding feature. The dorsal fin, which is long and narrow, can reach a height of 6 ft (1.8 m) above the body, whereas the female's fin seldom grows more than 3 ft (0.3 m). And finally it is worth noting that in reality the areas of pure white on the body can be altered. I once saw a pod of killer whales in Antarctic waters whose white markings were a delicate shade of green. The Norwegian skipper of our ship explained that this was because they had become stained with algae, commonly found at that time of the year in those latitudes.

In a diving manual published in 1963 the following advice appeared: 'The only treatment for being attacked by a killer whale

The killer whale, often known by the first part of its scientific name, simply as 'Orca', is in fact a large dolphin. Only its black upper surface shows here as it opens its blowhole to breath. Much of the lower body is white.

is reincarnation.' In other words, the general opinion among divers was that meeting a killer whale at close quarters was as lethal as finding yourself alone with a great white shark. Then, in 1964, something happened to challenge this idea. A killer whale was harpooned to serve as a model for a life-size sculpture in Vancouver's aquarium. The victim did not die, but was towed by a line attached to the harpoon in its back to Vancouver harbour where it was kept in a makeshift dock. The killer whale, which might have been expected to resent its treatment, swam docilely about its pool, exhibiting none of the fearsome behaviour formerly associated with the species. Thousands of people came to watch. The media even christened it Moby Doll. It settled down and after 55 days began to feed on 200 lb (90 kg) of fish a day, plus vitamin pills. The aquarium director, Dr Murray Newman, then began a scientific study of the sounds made by the killer whale. Unfortunately he was unable to continue for sufficient time to reach any conclusions, but it seemed highly likely that the captive was trying to communicate with others of its kind out at sea.

Sadly, Moby Doll died after 88 days in captivity. At the autopsy the whale was revealed to be a young male. If it was a typical killer whale, then the widely accepted image clearly needed to be

modified to include a gentle, highly sensitive pattern of behaviour. Sea parks and dolphinaria soon turned their attention to the possibility of adding killer whales to their cetacean entertainers.

Research into the vocalisations of killer whales continued around the coast where Moby Doll had been captured. In Georgia Strait off Vancouver Island, three scientists – Mike Bigg, Graeme Ellis, and John Ford – discovered three resident pods, each numbering between 80 and 90 animals. The one they called J-Pod spoke a dialect very like that of Moby Doll. Although the scientists' study was carried out 20 years after the captive's death, J-Pod was undoubtedly Moby Doll's family.

Further south, around the San Juan Islands between Vancouver and the Washington coast, an American scientist, Ken Balcomb, made regular contact with J-Pod. He plotted the group's southern movements, which were quite regular. They made the complete circuit between Vancouver Island and the San Juans every 10 days, ranging 200 miles (322 km). The members of J-Pod were extremely co-operative. Sometimes, when Balcomb went out in his boat searching for them, the pod would find him and put on a breaching and surface display, it is tempting to think, as a greeting. The structure of the pod was fairly typical: eight females with seven

A killer whale 'sounds' in the sunset off Vancouver Island. Scientists there have learned to distinguish members of the resident pods by the shapes of their fins.

169

A killer whale leaps above the water's surface showing its distinctive black and white markings.

calves of various ages and three adult males, all sons of the females.

Constant research enabled Bigg (in Canadian water) and Balcomb (in American waters) to name and identify all the members of the three resident pods. They identified them by the shape of their fins and their scars. As the result of these joint studies more was learned about killer whales in a few years than had been discovered in the past century. Killer whales, it emerged, may live in the wild for as long as 70 years. They have, however, a low rate of reproduction. On average, a female produces 1 calf every 10 years.

Killer whale pods have favourite fishing grounds, but there does not appear to be any sense of territoriality or rivalry. They usually fish as a family group, while at other times they gather in a super-pod, which may contain up to 90 members.

Studies conducted around Vancouver Island have revealed instances of strange, unexplained, whale behaviour. The discoverer was a pioneer in killer whale research, Ian MacAskey. In a remote bay – Robson's Bite at the northern end of the island – he found what he called 'the rubbing beach'. It was hidden away in a small cove. What attracts the killer whales to it, or why they behave as they do on arrival, remains a mystery. The water is not particularly clear. The bottom of the cove is covered in smooth flat stones, as are many other bays in the area. Some killer whales appear to 'drop in' when they are passing, while others come from long distances to visit the cove. But all of them behave in the same way on arrival – they rub themselves on the bottom pebbles, rather like a dog luxuriously scratching itself on a carpet. So far scientists have not found a satisfactory explanation for this behaviour. That it is something special is evident from the recordings made of the whales' voices – the sounds are quite unlike any of their usual vocalisations.

The most obvious explanation is that the whales are grooming themselves, dislodging irritating parasites against the bottom stones, but other coves are equally suitable for the purpose and are not used in this way. Some researchers think the significance is sexual or ritual, suggesting that young whales and their elders are taking part in an initiation or form of sexual education in the murky shallows. Such theories do seem to be carrying supposition beyond the bounds of reasonable scientific conjecture, although there is some evidence that the rubbing activity has a sexual aspect.

Unravelling the mysteries of killer whale communication is less difficult. Much of the work in this field has been done by John Ford, a Canadian biologist, working with Mike Bigg at the West Coast Whale Research Foundation. They have discovered that contact calls made when the whales are travelling are unique to each pod, suggesting a submarine flotilla operating on its own secret call sign. These signals are inherited by each successive generation.

Off Vancouver Island killer whale watching has become a popular pastime. Such public interest does not appear to disturb the killers and helps to increase sympathy for whales in general.

The intermittent clicking sounds made by all killer whales are used for echo-location, finding prey and identifying underwater objects – sight plays a secondary role. As in the great whales, a large part of the killer whale's, and indeed all dolphins', very large brain is concerned with interpreting the echoes from these clicks.

Occasionally, a family pod will rest on the surface. When it does so the voices change to a soft murmur, a sort of reassuring communal muttering. A family can rest like this for several hours, its members breathing every 30 seconds or so. In these relaxed periods the pod often dives together, swimming lazily underwater for five minutes at a time. The dreamy calls seem to co-ordinate these family dives, keeping the pod close together. There is no doubt that killer whales live a highly social and family-oriented life, though why this should be necessary for such a powerful creature that has no enemies is another mystery.

When the pod is fishing the calls take on a much more urgent pace and tone. This may be caused by excitement, or perhaps it is a way of keeping individual members of the pod in contact with each other. During the exhilaration of a chase among, for instance, a big shoal of homing salmon, individuals can wander miles from the rest of the pod. Although fishermen sometimes claim that the killers hunt as a team, driving the salmon into a tightly packed shoal, all the evidence suggests that each killer hunts for itself.

Most of the whale research has, for obvious reasons of accessibility and convenience, been carried out with resident pods. Yet researchers know of another type of killer whale that is less sociable than the members of the family pods, and approaches more closely the image of the deadly, silent killer. It is known as a 'transient'.

Transients appear briefly in the more sedentary pods' home ranges. About one third of the killer sightings recorded by scientists off Alaska are transients. They call very little, and when they do their voices are quite different from those of the family pods. Unlike the whales who live mainly on fish, these killers appear to feed largely on marine mammals. They are much less vocal when hunting, probably because marine mammals have ears. 'Radio' silence by the predators clearly pays off. Typically, they hunt around headlands and bays searching for unwary seals. Some scientists even wonder whether they may prove to be a sub-species. This, on the whole, seems unlikely. They are certainly less

A pod rests on the surface amid water vapour from one of its member's breathing. A family will sometimes rest like this for several hours and then, as if at a signal, all dive together.

approachable than the resident pods, but there have been no cases of aggression towards scientists attempting to study them. Nor is feeding on marine mammals exclusively a transient habit. Resident killer whales will prey on seal and sealions when fish is in short supply.

The most dramatic example of a family pod learning to catch marine mammals occurs in the far south of Argentina, at the headland Punta Norte, on the coast of Patagonia. The resident scientist, Juan Carlos Lopez, has become familiar with what would once have been considered very unusual killer whale behaviour. He continually studies several family pods that live and fish close inshore.

One particular family group is resident the entire year. It consists of a female with her calf, and a large adult with a slightly curved dorsal fin which makes him easily identifiable. The male does most of the hunting close inshore, while the family waits ¼ mile (0.4 km) out at sea. Usually he hunts for fish, but in March and April, when the growing sealion pups are becoming venturesome, he turns his attention to them.

The killer whale's image was further enhanced when, after 15 months' gestation, a female gave birth to a calf at Sea World seaquarium, San Diego. Calves had been born in captivity before but none had survived because the mother could not, or would not, feed them.

The killer has discovered a channel in the rock – the sealion pups are perfectly safe if they swim over the shallows on either side of it, but if they forget where they are, and venture over the deep water channel, the killer's sonar detects them. Not all his attacks are succcssful. The technique has clearly developed from normal inshore fishing methods, and has now become part of the killer whale's repertoire. Sometimes the female hunts over the rocky channel too.

Nearby is a colony of elephant seals. The killers' attack on their young is even more daring. Since the male killer whale is 27 ft (8.2 m) long, and weighs 6½ tonnes, reaching an elephant seal means the killer runs the risk of beaching itself. As usual, the victims are the unwary. Often they are immature bulls weighing

A killer whale's skull reveals teeth that close like a steel trap on fish, marine mammals or smaller cetaceans.

A most incredible sequence of pictures of a killer whale taking its victim out of a few inches of water on a lonely beach in Patagonia. The whale is 27 ft long and weighs six and a half tonnes. The victim, amazingly, does not see the attack coming until it is too late.

1,000–2,000 lb (453–907 kg). These juveniles are approaching the end of their first year, the time when they are starting to test their strength against rivals. They are not yet of mating age, and the contests are largely ritual in preparation for the real mating duels which will occur in two or three years' time. The battles, which often take place on the sand, almost in the surf, totally engage the young bulls' attention. This is exactly the right time for the killer whale to make an attack. The huge animal accelerates through the surf, smothered by spray, almost beaching itself. A fighting bull is seized so quickly you can barely see what happens in the burst of exploding white water. The killer carries the live seal in its jaws 1,200 ft (365 m) to its waiting family. Lopez believes that the male often gives the struggling seal to its young as a practice kill.

Following Moby Doll's captivity in Vancouver harbour, several killer whales were captured to be exhibited in dolphinaria. Perhaps the most notable is Sea World in San Diego. Here the centrepiece is the Shamu Stadium where the killer whales put on their show

At considerable risk of beaching itself, the killer whale grabs its meal. Then it turned in a smother of spray and took the still struggling creature out to its female and calf who were waiting off-shore.

In seaquaria, killer whales have proved co-operative, friendly and highly trainable although their keepers say that the whales teach them the routines: should such large wild creatures be submitted to life in captivity, however good the conditions?

twice a day. The Sea World trainers have been able to establish an amazing rapport with the whales. In fact they have said that the performances are almost invariably based on the whales' 'ideas' rather than their own. These ideas come from daily activity sessions which include play, exercise, learning, and socialising with their individual trainers. The whales show what they like doing best, and these 'tricks' are often included in their performances.

However, such shows prompted fierce debate about the ethics of keeping these great animals in captivity, and making them part of an aquatic circus. Are they tormented prisoners slowly going mad in the echoing confines of their pools? Or are they well-fed, fit, contented creatures who really enjoy the richness and variety of their new if artificial life? While the argument continues, many dolphinaria and seaquariums have decided not to put killer whales on show.

What is unarguable, though, is that the killer whale's appearance in some entertainment centres has entirely changed its once deadly image. In the public's mind, the killer whale has ceased to be the dreaded sea demon to be bracketed with 'Jaws'. Killer whales have become warm, responsive and kindly creatures of great grace and skill. This image was greatly enhanced when, after 15 months' gestation, a female gave birth at Sea World to a calf, named Shamu after her father. While baby killer whales had previously been born in captivity, in each case the calf died because the mother could not or would not feed it. Yet within days Shamu was swimming strongly round her pool with her parents. (And, incidentally if, as seems likely, more and more countries ban the capture of killer whales within their waters, future displays in seaquaria will depend entirely on the success of captive breeding programmes.)

The great whales have won public sympathy and even some measure of government support in most countries. Now the dolphins are in equal need of international understanding and protective legislation. Every year hundreds of thousands of dolphins drown when caught in nylon tuna nets. Also, mass ritual slaughters are carried out when dolphin species, such as pilot whales, annually strand themselves. They are hacked to death for no better reason than that the killings are traditional. The Japanese, who are insatiable eaters of whale meat, have turned their attention to the smaller cetaceans now that their 'scientific' cull of minke whales has been limited. They are now even killing porpoises, which strictly speaking are not dolphins but belong to the family *Phocoenidae*. As far as the Japanese are concerned, the classification does not matter. What counts is that even porpoises can provide between 100–200 lb (45–90 kg) of 'whale meat'.

It is ironic that mankind should ever have attached the prefix 'killer' to *Orcinus orca* in view of his treatment of the whale's smaller relatives. So far orca has escaped the killing, but who would like to guarantee even the killer whale's future?

The Seas Must Live

In the mid 1970s the World Wildlife Fund, as it was then known, ran a campaign to focus the world's attention on the extent to which we are destroying the oceans. The campaign – The Seas Must Live – succeeded in that aim and raised funds to help tackle the many difficult problems awaiting a solution. What was at stake was nearly two thirds of the surface of the planet, and every living creature in those waters. More than 10 years later we have made some progress towards healing some of the more superficial 'wounds' we continually inflict on the sea. We have, so to speak, bandaged a few cuts. The general health of the patient, however, has not greatly improved.

Part of the problem, ironically, seems to have stemmed from such notions as the 'freedom of the seas'. Originally the phrase implied freedom to navigate the oceans. The only seas that were the property of maritime nations were those known as territorial waters, and their limit was set at 3 miles (5 km) offshore. This distance was the maximum range of a cannon shot, and beyond that no maritime nation had any jurisdiction. Beyond the limit anyone could do as they liked, and sadly they increasingly did so. Freedom of the seas has consequently meant the freedom to dump anything in the sea, the freedom to pollute it and cause irrevocable damage.

Until a century ago it was unthinkable that we could damage the kingdom of the deep. The seas were so wide, so deep, and so blue that it seemed nothing we could do could ever hurt them. That blue surface is such a beautiful cover it is easy to forget the crimes against nature that it conceals. If only one could pull the plug out of

Sea and land are closely interlocked in one huge ecosystem, encapsulated here in this picture of a gull snatching squid from the water.

A red tide. Sometimes these swarms of single-celled dino-flagellates occur naturally. They can also be stimulated by some of the fertilisers which we increasingly pour into the oceans. Red tides can prove poisonous to fish and birds and even to people who eat sea food affected by them.

the bottom of the Atlantic Ocean and explore the sea bed. What would we find? How much evidence would there be of pollution?

Heading east from New York, we must first cross the shallow continent shelf. It is 200 miles (322 km) wide and possibly the most ill-treated piece of ocean in the world. This is where New York throws its garbage. And at the top of the deep chasm, Hudson Canyon, there is a dumping ground for demolition debris. A little further out to sea there is an acid waste dump. Where the canyon drops off into deep water a large area of the seabed is allocated for chemical wastes and inactive explosives. Further out there are even more explosive dumps. And that is not the end of it. As in the North Sea there is oil under this shelf, so there is the possibility of additional pollution from future drilling sites.

Moving down the continental slope, which falls off quite steeply from a depth of 656 ft (200 m) to as much as 3,827 ft (3,500 m), huge peaks loom up. They are the New England Sea Mounts, rearing 3 miles (4.8 km) high. Bermuda, to the far south, is the tiny tip of a similar sea mount, just sticking above the surface.

As we travel further towards mid-ocean, we pass even more sea mounts. They are made of solid basalt, unlike any other mountains on the surface of the planet. We then approach a mountain range that makes the Himalayas look puny and the Grand Canyon a mere ditch. We are entering the Mid-Atlantic Ridge, a curving spine 12,000 miles (19,311 km) long, many of whose peaks dwarf the Alps. The main canyon is 130 miles (209 km) wide, and every 40–50 miles (65–80 km) it is split by cross canyons. These fractures stretch for hundreds, sometimes thousands, of miles on either side. This ridge is where four of the tectonic plates on which the continents sit (see Chapter Four) are pulling themselves apart. There is no erosion in these depths and so the towering slopes on either side of this immense rift are quite smooth. Huge fractured blocks on the canyon floor look as new as the day the lava welled up to form them. Some of the other lava boulders are a weird shape. They are what is known as 'pillow lava'. The molten magma gushing out at 2,000 degrees Farenheit has cooled rapidly in the ice-cold water and formed a hard outer skin inside which still molten lava has imploded and exploded until it, too, has cooled, leaving the pillow-shaped volcanic boulder.

A rockhopper colony in stormy seas; giant strands of kelp can be seen lying over the slabs of rock which form the penguins' home. Such a scene is only possible in a healthy ocean.

The journey across the emptied seabed continues westward over a thousand miles towards the African coast. We are travelling across the abyssal plain until we reach the continental slope rising to the shelf again, a replica of the formations we left behind on the New England coast of the USA.

Now, let's put the imaginary plug back in the bottom of the Atlantic again and allow the water to fill it so that we can see what lives in and over the strange landscape we have traversed.

The shallow continental shelves – generally agreed to extend to depths of 200 metres – are not only the most abused part of the ocean, they are also the most productive. Here we come to an immediate contradiction in man's behaviour towards the waters that lie over the shelves. He wants the maximum food yield from them in terms of fish. (The seas, incidentally, produce 70 million tons of food annually, much of which comes from these continental waters.) To get this maximum yield, the maritime nations frequently overfish the shelves. This has to be counter-productive in the long run. Not only that, but those same nations pollute the shallow seas with effluents from their rivers to the detriment of everything living in them, including valuable commercial food fish.

As an example, it was recently calculated that the Mediterranean is being polluted each year with: 12,000 tonnes of oil; 60,000 tonnes of detergent; 100 tonnes of mercury; 3,800 tonnes of lead; 2,400 tonnes of chromnium; and 21,000 tonnes of zinc.

Another problem is the way in which maritime nations arbitrarily alter the boundaries of their territorial waters and therefore fishing zones. In the 1970s Iceland declared that no one could fish within 200 miles (321 km) of her shores. This unilateral decision resulted

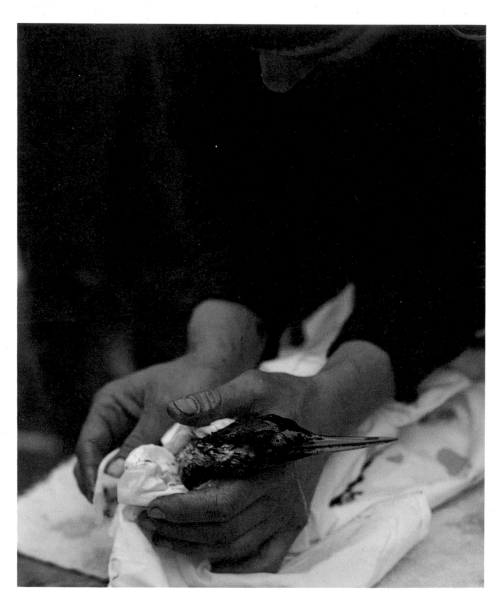

A bird harmed by oil pollution. Will it ever stop? Probably not so long as there is oil to be drilled and tankers to carry it on the high seas.

in the so-called 'cod-war', with Icelandic fishery patrol boats and British frigates daily in near conflict. Where national interests are concerned it has so far proved impossible to thrash out a fishing policy to which all will agree.

The continental shelves are also the areas where oil spills most usually occur. Sadly, they are also the part of the sea where millions of gallons of crude oil will inflict the most damage on fishery, recreational, and wildlife interests. An oiled seabird is invariably a dead bird. If the spill happens in the summer months when millions of auks, kittiwakes, gulls and petrels have sought land to breed, then the damage to these species may take years to overcome. Tragically, in some cases the species never recover.

The causes of the spills are almost invariably navigational and happen mainly in crowded shipping lanes, despite modern navigational aids. Perhaps, however, they are not so surprising when you realize that a big tanker can take 5 miles (8 km) to stop. It should be possible to provide a traffic control system in narrow waters like the English Channel, similar to that given to aircraft approaching and leaving an international airport. Yet skippers are reluctant to let anyone else, figuratively speaking, have a hand on the helm. Alternatively, why could not tankers be better constructed, for example with a double-skinned hull, to reduce the likelihood of an oil spill after a collision. One of the worst of the recent instances of oil pollution concerned the *Exxon Valdez*. In March 1989, the ship hit rocks in the unspoilt waters of Prince William Sound, the narrow inlet that leads to the Alaskan oil terminal at Valdez. A quarter of a million barrels of crude oil polluted the sea. The senior vice-president of the oil company Exxon described the disaster as 'a highly unlikely spill. After 12 years of production the efficiency of the terminal has been 99.995 per cent, which is better than most human endeavours.'

Too little and far too late. The oil booms go out in Prince Rupert Sound in an attempt to collect the crude oil shed by the Exxon Valdes, *but the damage has been done.*

KINGDOM OF THE DEEP

Amid this woolly-minded playing with statistics, he had clearly forgotten the appalling damage that could result from the 0.005 per cent of terrifying inefficiency. 'Highly unlikely' it may have been, but it happened. It is estimated that 3,000 sea otters died, and an incalculable number of seabirds, possibly as many as 20,000. In addition there are the long-term effects of the spill that are likely to be the most serious consequences. Fishing, a key Alaskan industry on that part of the coast, will be ruined for years to come. The small marine creatures on which fish feed were substantially wiped out by the oil, which oozed out of the Sound westwards down the Kenai Peninsular, continuing its evil work. Fortunately the Sound's 160 killer whales, all members of the resident pods, left the area before they became engulfed in the oil.

If the continental shelves suffer from most of mankind's worst excesses, the largest ocean areas of all, the middle seas, are by no means immune. These are the endless stretches of sea that lie neither over the great deeps nor the shallow shelves. They do not particularly abound in fish life, and were once the playground of the great whales, rarely seen here now in large numbers. A measure of the vastness of the middle seas can be gauged from the absence of a starling-sized seabird, the storm petrel. This tiny bird, named after St Peter because when feeding it appears to walk on the water, is said to be the most numerous species in the world. Yet you can voyage around the globe and only see very small numbers of them above the middle seas. The world's most numerous seabird is made to seem scarce by the immensity of the area in which it lives.

You might think that these limitless and distant areas of sea would be too far from shore to be damaged by pollution. On his voyage across the south Pacific on the raft Kon-Tiki, the explorer and writer Thor Heyerdhal took daily water samples. He found that no part of the great expanse of water that the expedition's raft crossed was free from droplets of oil. Too often the middle seas, well out of sight of land and other ships, are where unscrupulous tanker captains, in defiance of all laws and regulations, wash out their tanks. They do so to avoid 'wasting' time and their company's money cleaning their tanks with the proper facilities when they dock.

Beyond the middle seas are the deeps. For a long time no one knew how deep was the ocean. On its remarkable circumnavigation in 1872, the research ship *Challenger* recorded depths of 26,850 (8 km) in the Pacific. She did so by the time-honoured method of lowering a weight at the end of a calibrated line. In 1960 Jacques Piccard, with an American navy man Don Walsh, took a bathyscaphe *Trieste* (bathyscaphe comes from the Greek words for deep and small boat) down into the deepest pit, in the deepest trench, in the deepest part of any ocean. This was the Challenger Deep in the Marianas Trench in the Pacific. They touched the bottom at a depth of 7 miles (11 km). Piccard records how, as the bathyscaphe neared the seabed, 'I saw a wonderful thing. Lying on the bottom just beneath us was some type of flatfish, resembling a sole, about one foot long and six inches across.'

Many explorations of the deep have since been made in other submersibles. In the Galapagos rift hot volcanic springs have been found to support oases of life 1½ miles (2.4 km) down, including populations of crabs and tube worms. Further research has revealed that there is an astonishing amount of life at these great depths. However it is so extremely thinly spread out that a trawl the size of a living room has to be pulled through 10 miles (16 km) of the abyss in order to produce just one bucketful of the strange creatures who live there.

Many animals of the deep, such as squid, shrimp and jellyfish, migrate towards the surface at night, though how they manage to

Perhaps we would understand more about the Kingdom of the Deep if we could pull the plug out of the oceans and let the water temporarily drain away. Peter Parks of Oxford Scientific Films built a model of the Atlantic seabed to depict just that situation. Behind the camera in New York, in the foreground the mid-Atlantic ridge.

withstand the changes in pressure is one of the deep seas' many mysteries. These nocturnal concentrations are often called deep scattering layers because of the way they disrupt sonar readings. Another mystery is why many of the animals of the abyss are coloured red when they live in a world where there is not sufficient light to distinguish one colour from another. Also, some creatures have huge complex eyes which appear redundant. *Gigantocypris*, a relative of the shrimp, has eyes like car reflectors. Yet it does not need eyes to catch its food since it is a filter-feeder, and is too slow-moving to avoid predators, even if it could see them coming.

Many of the animals that live in near or total darkness use luminosity either to find mates, lure prey, or frighten predators. A 1 ft (0.3048 km) fish called *Stomias* has a row of luminous spots along its flank, whose purpose is uncertain. What is clear, however, is the use to which it puts the luminous lantern sticking out of its lower jaw.

It lures prey fish. *Stomias* is big by deep-sea standards. Because of the harsh conditions and shortage of food, few deep-water creatures grow to more than several inches long. There is, however, one shark that hunts on the bottom of the Pacific. The cat shark is the grand total of 8 in (20 cm) long.

At present it seems that mankind can find no special use for the oceans' depths or the animals that live there, other than using the trenches as dumping grounds for lethal compounds which cannot be stored safely elsewhere. Yet even here there are problems. Some containers have later been washed ashore. In fact we know so little about deep sea currents that Davey Jones' deepest locker may not be nearly so secure as we think. We run the risk that the deadly garbage we believe has been disposed of forever may leak, fatally damaging the fragile eco-systems of which we know so little, and which one day we may wish to use constructively.

The deep ocean floor contains one kind of wealth that is possibly exploitable. In the 1960s, manganese nodules were regarded as a new form of wealth. The deep Pacific seabed was said to be littered with such nodules and other precious minerals, varying in size from a small round pebble to a cannon ball. Some people believed there was instant wealth if only it could be brought to the surface. Yet since the nodules were lying 12,000–15,000 ft (3.6–4.5 m) down, there were clearly major problems.

The nodules certainly existed, and had been photographed. How they had accreted was a mystery, the most likely explanation being that the minerals precipitated from the sea water around a nucleus that might be a fish tooth, a small piece of volcanic debris, or dead coral. The nodules, it has to be said, are not a new discovery. The research ship *Challenger* dredged some up in 1872. It was the discovery of their abundance that fired get-rich-quick imaginations in the 1960s.

Most of the nodules are still down there. One day they may be brought to the surface in economic quantities. Pilot experiments, however, have revealed a range of difficulties in addition to those of raising them. Even in quite small areas the mineral content and quality of the metal in the nodules is not consistent, and therefore makes any costing and estimate of likely profits extremely difficult. The average ore content is not as high as expected. Even so, it is sufficiently big to interest a few major consortia who have the money and the expertise to tackle the job. One typical nodule contains 27–30 per cent manganese, 1.1–1.4 per cent nickel, 1–1.3 per cent copper, and 0.2–0.4 per cent cobalt.

It could be argued that the story of the possible mineral riches hidden in the ocean depths does not have a place in a book whose main concern is the oceans and their inhabitants. That would be true but for one point. The 'Deep Sea Bubble' concerning sea bed minerals inflated almost to bursting point in the 1960s. The developing nations, and particularly those without a sea coast, feared that this great wealth would be grabbed by the technically developed nations under the traditional doctrine of the 'freedom of the seas'. Who, they asked, owns the ocean once you sail beyond territorial waters? Should not the wealth that lies hidden there belong to all mankind rather than to the first technical buccaneers who want to exploit it? It was a good and fair question then, and it is an even more relevant one now.

Such questions led to the creation of the United Nations Seabed Committee in 1967. A Declaration of Principles, approved by UNO's General Assembly in 1970, declared that beyond the limits of national jurisdiction (which were not defined) lies an area of ocean that no state may legally appropriate. This area was described as 'the common heritage of all mankind', and was to be subject to regulations drawn up by an international body. Since then there have been several Law of the Sea Conventions. Many useful interstate agreements have been reached, but they are local successes, and cannot replace an internationally accepted Law of the Sea. Everyone agrees that the day when freedom of the seas means a free-for-all beyond territorial waters has long passed. But if we cannot arrive at an international law of the sea, binding on all nations, then we are on the way to damaging what is certainly the most important two thirds of our planet. And yet the problems facing the law makers are immensely complex, far more so than any comparable laws relating to *terra firma*. The conflicting interests are numerous: military, fishing, mineral exploitation, oil, shipping, territorial and environmental. The latter is certainly the most important of all.

The astronauts, referred to at the very start of this book, who described earth from the far side of space as the 'Blue Planet', reminded us of the seas' potential beauty. Unwittingly, they also reminded us of the extent to which huge areas of sea are tragically no longer pure and blue. The oceans, on which our future depends, are sick. Fortunately for mankind they have enormous powers of recovery, but covering nearly two thirds of the planet's surface they will require all the help all the nations on the planet can give them.

More than any other creature, the dolphin symbolises the freedom and riches of the deep. Mankind has always had a special regard for these highly intelligent marine mammals. Let us hope that this regard will be increasingly extended towards the oceans and the animals that depend upon them.

Index

190